V. V. Vinogradov

GOGOL
and the
Natural School

Translated by Debra K. Erickson and Ray Parrott

Introduction by Debra K. Erickson

Ardis Essay Series, No. 7

Ardis, Ann Arbor

V. V. Vinogradov, *Gogol and the Natural School*
Copyright © 1987 by Ardis Publishers
All rights reserved under International and Pan-American Copyright Conventions.
Printed in the United States of America

Translated from the original Russian

Ardis Publishers
2901 Heatherway
Ann Arbor, Michigan 48104

Library of Congress Cataloging in Publication Data

Vinogradov, V. V. (Viktor Vladimirovich), 1895-1969.
    Gogol and the natural school.

    Translation of: Gogol' i natural'naia shkola.
    1. Gogol', Nikolai Vasil'evich, 1809-1852—
Criticism and interpretation. I. Title.
PG3335.Z8V5313   1987   891.78'309   86-22239

ISBN 0-87501-008-3 (alk. paper)

Contents

Part One: Introduction: V. V. Vinogradov	7
Biography	9
Vinogradov and the Formalists	11
The Division of Belles Lettres	11
Perceptions Regarding Vinogradov and the Formalists	12
Formalist Theory	14
Vinogradov's Views	17
V. V. Vinogradov's "Gogol and the Natural School"	22
Notes	26
Bibliography	28
Part Two: Gogol and the Natural School	29
Chapter 1	31
Chapter 2	45
Chapter 3	55
Chapter 4	65
Chapter 5	85
Notes	93

Part One

Introduction: V. V. Vinogradov

Biography

The author of "Gogol and the Natural School" (*Gogol' i Natural'naia Shkola,* 1925), Viktor Vladimirovich Vinogradov, was a Soviet linguist and literary scholar best known for his studies on the Russian literary language and its history. His work was not confined to these areas, however. Between the beginning of his research career in the late 1910s and his death in 1969, Vinogradov produced studies on such diverse topics as Russian grammar and lexicology, the poetics of individual writers of medieval and modern times, and a history of the literary language.[1]

As a novice literary scholar Vinogradov relied primarily on the methods of linguistics in undertaking the "immanent" study of literature, an approach which had been fitfully developing for over half a century before his career began. Employing this approach, he devoted most of the first decade of his career (the 1920s) to the study of the poetics of individual writers and literary schools. The works of Gogol, Dostoevsky and the "Natural School" were his major interest at this time.

From the late 1920s until the mid-1930s Vinogradov elaborated general theories of literary language, but soon returned his attention to the work of individual writers, confining himself almost solely to questions of style. During the next two decades he produced studies on the poetics of writers including Krylov, Karamzin, Pushkin, Lermontov and Turgenev. During his final years, Vinogradov's work in literary studies centered largely around the theory of literary language.

Vinogradov's work was not confined to literary study. In addition to conducting research on a broad range of linguistic topics, Vinogradov maintained an active career in teaching and academic administration. During his life he wrote and published numerous books and journal articles.[2] He received numerous awards, including the Stalin Prize[3] and the Order of Lenin.[4]

Vinogradov displayed an orientation toward a high level of diverse and intense activity even in his earliest years. Born in Zaraisk in the province of Riazan in 1895, Vinogradov moved to Petrograd after receiving a secondary education in the seminary in his native city. In the capital he entered historical-philological and archeological institutes, and was selected for preparatory programs leading to professorship in each upon being graduated in 1917. He was chosen for a similar position at Petrograd University in 1919, the same year in which he became a teacher at a women's pedagogical institute. In 1921 he was appointed to a teaching post at Petrograd State University and became an associate in the State Institute of the History of the Arts. Voted an active member in 1924, Vinogradov served as chairman of this Institute's Section of Artistic Speech between 1925 and 1929.[5]

In 1930 Vinogradov moved to Moscow where, after serving briefly as a teacher at a pedagogical institute, he accepted a position in the Subdivision of Russian Language in the Department of Philology at Moscow University. He served as chairman of the Subdivision of Russian Language from 1945 until his death.[6]

After being appointed an academician of the Academy of Sciences of the USSR in 1946, Vinogradov was elected to numerous administrative posts. He directed the Academy's Institute of Linguistics between 1950 and 1954, and its Institute of Russian Language between 1958 and 1968. He served as academician-secretary of the Department of Literature and Language from 1950 until 1963, and headed the section of Historical Poetics and Stylistics of Russian Classical Literature from 1968 until his death.[7]

Vinogradov and the Formalists

The Division of Belles Lettres

Most of Vinogradov's scholarly activity of the 1920s, the period in which he wrote "Gogol and the Natural School," was associated with the newly established Division of Belles Lettres at the State Institute of History of the Arts in Petrograd.[8]

It was partly through his activity in this institute that Vinogradov came to be associated with the "Formalists," those literary scholars who, in polemical and scholarly activity between 1914 and the late 1920s, set forth much of the theoretical framework and practical models for the "scientific," i.e., intrinsic study of literature. More specifically, these scholars sought to define the essence of literature in order to undertake its objective study and discover the peculiarly literary laws determining its construction and evolution.

The Formalists' practice of treating literature as an "immanent phenomenon" ran counter to the dominant traditions of the preceding century, during which literature had been examined as a historical-cultural, philosophical, or psycho-biographical document.

When the leaders of the Petrograd wing of the Formalist movement—V. B. Shklovsky, B. M. Eikhenbaum and Iu. N. Tynianov—entered the Division of Belles Lettres in the early 1920s it became the unofficial center for Formalist activities. Prior to this, their work, which had been predominated by polemics, was formulated and published by an informal circle, The Society of Poetic Language, known by the acronym Opojaz. Once established within the Institute, the Formalists largely were able to forgo polemics and engage in concrete research.[9]

The Division of Belles Lettres was formed in November 1920 to fulfill tasks in keeping with Formalist theory. In its statement of purpose, the division declared: "Up until now the study of literary movements has suffered from an unprincipled eclecticism of methods: the poetic work has been examined at one moment as the material for a world view and at another as an historical-cultural factor and so forth... The Institute of the Arts, in keeping with its special task, should approach literature as a literary art. Here, as in other departments of the Institute, creative (and in this particular case—poetic) devices in their historical development and the history of the creative (poetic) style as an integral whole or system of creative devices serve as the method of study."[10]

The Institute's influence over the work of its members was enhanced by its practice of requiring that all works published under its auspices first be presented before a general session of its members for discussion and criticism. Two of Vinogradov's works, "Studies on Gogol's Style" (*Etiudy o stile Gogolia*, 1926) and "The Evolution of Russian Naturalism" (*Evoliutsiia russkogo naturalizma*, 1929), and two of his articles, "The Problem of Skaz in Stylistics" ("Problema skaza v stilistike," 1926) and "On the Construction of a Theory of Poetic Language" ("K postroeniiu teorii poeticheskogo iazyka," 1927), passed through this crucible.[11]

Although Vinogradov's work was never published in any of the Opojaz materials, he did become associated with the new circle which the Opojaz members established within the Institute.[12] In becoming associated with the Formalists, Vinogradov adopted—in addition to their terminology—their approach of treating literature as an immanent series. He also addressed similar topics.

Perceptions Regarding Vinogradov and the Formalists

Although Vinogradov's work of the early 1920s reflected the approach and concerns of the Formalists, he did not perceive himself, nor is he perceived by most scholars, as a Formalist.[13] In his *Russian Formalism*, Victor Erlich describes Vinogradov as a "quasi-Formalist" and speaks of his "explorations of Gogol and the so-called 'Natural School'" as "near-Formalist contributions."[14] In his examination of the evolution of the

Formalist movement in the article "The Theory of the Formal Method" ("Teoriia formal'nogo metoda," 1924), Boris M. Eikhenbaum places five of Vinogradov's articles published between 1922 and 1924 in the same general category with other Formalist studies of literary evolution, while granting that they were "not directly tied to Opojaz."[15]

Whether or not Vinogradov was a Formalist in the proper sense, he is nearly always discussed in conjunction with the Formalists and his work in the 1920s was replete with Formalist influences. As R. Lachmann noted in her study on Vinogradov, "As concerns the early Vinogradov's conceptual apparatus, methods, and objectives, they are on the same plane as Iakubinsky's, Larin's, Eikhenbaum's, and Iakobson's."[16]

That Vinogradov should have chosen to minimize the relationship in subsequent years is not surprising in light of the political persecution the movement suffered from the late 20s through the mid-50s for its "reactionary"[17] tendencies and sympathy for "pseudo-innovative"[18] modernist art. All of the Formalists found it necessary to reorient their work (or emigrate) and a few were forced to recant.[19] During this period the word "Formalist" became a label of opprobrium, and to this day still carries negative connotations in the Soviet Union.[20]

But much of the bad press that Formalism has received has been directed toward genuine weaknesses of the movement. Having set about to identify the intrinsic features of verbal art, the Formalists displayed a proclivity to reduce literary art to these features alone, to equate literature with "literariness," i.e., features peculiar to literature.[21]

Furthermore, the preoccupation with the verbal nature of literature—which had brought this band of linguists and literary scholars together in the first place—led them in the early years to downplay the significance of all but the linguistic features of the literary work.[22]

Once the Formalists made it through these early stages, however, they emerged with a distilled and much improved theory of literature, a theory from which Vinogradov was to reap much benefit.

Formalist Theory

More than anything else, what the Formalists brought to literary studies was an acute sense of form and function. During the early years of the movement it was form that stood foremost in these young scholars' minds, but every advance made in their conception of form underscored the significance of function.

The assertion of the nineteenth-century Russian-Ukrainian philologist Alexander Potebnia that "prose and poetry are linguistic material"[23] prompted literary scholars to turn to linguistics to help them study this basic formal feature of the literary work. Relying on linguistic concepts elaborated by the German semasiologist Edmund Husserl in their attempts to define "poetic" language, these scholars noted that its distinction lay in its function.[24] Quite unlike the word in "practical" language which served to convey information about its denotatum, the "poetic" word tended to beg attention.[25] As opposed to the neutral character of the "practical" word, the "poetic" word was marked, and in this lay its primary value. As the Futurists, the most influential poets of the period, said, the "poetic" word was "self-valuable."[26]

When the Formalists became organized at this time, this concept lay at the base of their campaign to elevate form from its subordination to content. Basic to the Formalists' developing view of art was the idea that form determined content, rather than the converse.[27]

The preoccupation with the literary work's perceptible features, which this concept engendered, led to the development of a new aesthetic which one Marxist critic of the Formalists, P. N. Medvedev, called "psycho-physiological."[28] The Formalists thought that man had a basic need for the process of perceiving; so above all, it was the task of art to "make [things] perceptible."[29]

Medvedev considered this principle the "cornerstone" of Formalism because it was the factor the Formalists saw as determining, not only the construction of the individual work of art, but the course of literary history as well.[30]

But the importance of this principle can only be considered in light of the Formalists' view of the composition of literature. They asserted that the components of literature made up a relatively limited repertory, and that contrary to most views, the artist did not dream up new forms to convey new concepts, but reworked and reassembled the components of the repertory to create aesthetic effects; and only novelty could insure such effects. To create effects, the artist strove to impede automatic reactions. He made his depictions difficult, so that the perceiver would become aware of form. This deliberate obfuscation, which was generally effected by "shifting" objects onto a "new semantic plane," was called the device of "estrangement."[31]

In essence, the device of estrangement is nothing other than one of the long-recognized features of art—the tendency toward innovation. It long has been noted that art strives to place the familiar in a new light. What was novel about the Formalists' view was that the innovative impulse was concentrated in the formal features of the work, rather than in its content. This conception deprived content of its weight; it became largely a reflection of form.

Because language was the first formal feature to which the Formalists' attention was drawn, they spent their early years trying to demonstrate its independent value. Owing partly to their alliance with the Futurist poets whose poetry had a pure sound, "trans-sense" orientation, and partly to their desire to illustrate their newly devised concept of the "perceptible verbal construction" of the poetic language, the Formalists became preoccupied with the acoustic features of the literary work.[32]

In the late 1910s, however, the Formalists began to examine the morphology of the literary text, elaborating theories on the functions of various elements which they investigated. Though the sphere of their investigation widened, their studies suffered from the tendency to view all of a work's formal features as functions of whichever feature they happened to be studying.

This tendency was particularly pronounced, for example, in such works as B. M. Eikhenbaum's "How Gogol's 'The

Overcoat' Is Made" ("Kak sdelana 'Shinel' ' Gogolia," 1919) where all constructional elements are seen as products of the author's preoccupation with sound, and his *The Young Tolstoi* (*Molodoi Tolstoi*, 1922) and V. Shklovsky's *The Unraveling of the Plot* (*Razvertyvanie siuzheta*, 1921), "The Plot in Dostoevsky's Work" ("Siuzhet u Dostoevskogo," 1921) and *Rozanov* ("Rozanov", 1921) where all formal features tend to be reduced to exigencies of plot development or parody.

Although the Formalists were inclined to exaggerate the relative importance of certain features, they were beginning to develop a view of the work as a system. As B. M. Eikhenbaum said:

> A work of art is always the product of a complex conflict between formative elements, always a kind of compromise. The elements do not simply coexist and do not simply 'correspond' to each other. Depending on the general character of the style some element or other operates as an organizing *dominant*, prevailing over the others and subjugating them to itself.[33]

In addition to noting the close interrelationships within individual works, the Formalists noted the relationships between works and began to develop an understanding of the processes of literary history. While they, like their predecessors, examined "borrowings" and "sources," they were more interested in the new meaning or effect generated by the transfer and new treatment of literary material. One device which was much discussed in this connection was the basic technique of parody, "baring the device."[34] This involved the artist's appropriation of a conventional literary technique or one characteristically used by an individual writer and employing it in such a deliberately awkward or inappropriate fashion that its presence, which had perhaps become indiscernible in other contexts, became immediately apparent. The Formalists' awareness of this device predisposed them to see it perhaps too frequently. As mentioned before, they tended to grant too much importance to each new device they identified.

All the same, they did notice that the relationships between works, the forces governing literary history, were various. As V. Shklovsky wrote in 1921:

> The work of art is perceived as the background and by means of association with other works of art. The form of a work of art is determined by its relationship to other previously existing forms. The material of a work of art is necessarily loud-pedalled, i.e. marked out, "voiced." Not only parody, but in general any work of art is created as a parallel and contradiction to a model. A new form appears not in order to express new content, but to replace an old form which has lost its artistic value.[35]

During this period the Formalists were more or less concerned with developing a general theory of literature, at least partly so that they could distinguish between the literary and non-literary and find a scientific i.e., objective way of approaching literature as an immanent series.[36]

Although they did discover some basic literary functions and came to see the formal features of a work as comprising both an inter- and intra-textual system, they had been dealing with generalities, rather than particulars. They had generated a theory of literature but had not yet really begun to establish the poetics of individual writers and trace the course of literary history.

Vinogradov's Views

For Vinogradov, as for many of the Formalists, establishing the poetics of individual writers presented itself as a task of the first order in the early 1920s. And while he shared Formalist views about the nature of the literary work, he saw his task as a theoretician somewhat differently. Having been trained as a historical linguist and influenced by his teacher-mentor, A. A. Shakhmatov, who was renowned for having reconstructed various ancient dialects, Vinogradov had similarly broad aims. He wanted to establish the literary language of various writers, periods, and epochs.[37]

Like the Formalists, he thought that linguistics would

serve as a good tool for the tasks of establishing poetics; but unlike many of them, he did not think that the linguist's task should be confined to the identification and classification of forms. He thought that stylistic analysis, the task he had set for himself, should base itself in semantics.[38]

Vinogradov outlined his approach in a 1923 article, "On the Tasks of Stylistics. Observations on the Life of the Archpriest Avvakum" ("O zadachakh stilistiki. Nabliudeniia nad stilem protopopa Avvakuma"). Unlike the Formalists, who up until that time had been inclined to start with theory first, Vinogradov advocated an approach which started from the bottom, analyzing the smallest units of meaning in the text (symbolics)[39] and working up to the principles underlying their disposition (syntactics).[40] Architectonics,[41] the level on which separate stylistic spheres are conjoined to make a plot, appears in later analyses, including "Gogol and the Natural School."

Although the Formalists had been discussing literature as a system, Vinogradov's training enabled him to treat it as such perhaps before any of the Formalists did. Taking their lead from the French linguist Ferdinand de Saussure who adjured his students to confine themselves to synchronic studies of language, many Russian literary scholars insisted that historical poetics was an anachronism. Others, and Vinogradov cited B. M. Eikhenbaum and V. V. Zhirmunsky among them in his discussion of synchronic and diachronic study (functional-immanent and retrospective-projected, as he termed them), were not careful to observe the distinction, a fact which made their studies "methodologically unsatisfactory."[42] Vinogradov noted that although the two methods might be used complementarily, a failure to keep the existence of the two planes in mind caused scholars to exaggerate the significance of either inter- or intra-textual dynamics.

Addressing methodological issues involved in concrete studies in his article "On the Tasks of Stylistics," Vinogradov acknowledges the establishment of historical poetics as a distant aim, but insists on the necessity of first establishing the styles of individual writers.[43] This was to commence with the synchronic examination of individual works after which, having considered them from the standpoint of chronology, a generalization about the writer's style as a dynamic system or structure could be drawn. Only from this point could the influence of broader spheres—those of schools and epochs—be considered. One year after completing "Gogol and the Natural School" he wrote, "The question of borrowings should be replaced by the question of 'structural possibilities'."[44] It was only after understanding the basic character of an author's style that the true function of borrowed elements could be considered.

In this same article, Vinogradov's earliest program for stylistic analysis, he makes the rather unexpected recommendation that the scholar not avoid seeking to define the "transforming personality"[45] which determined the disposition of elements in the text. It was the scholar's task "to find the system linking the choice of words and . . . syntactical series by inner psychological unity and through this glimpse the means of the aesthetic formation of the verbal material."[46]

After applying this approach in a subsequent analysis of Akhmatova's poetry, Vinogradov met with great criticism from the Formalists who perceived it as psychologism.[47] Vinogradov, however, continued to defend the need for establishing the writer's "poetic" or "linguistic consciousness"[48] which he saw as a means of discovering the connecting thread or inner logic of a writer's work. This concept was not so much tied to the writer's psychology as it was to the aesthetic impulse or authorial intent underlying the work.

The term "linguistic consciousness," however, which embraced this concept of the "transforming personality," included still another concept which was to supercede the first in importance in Vinogradov's subsequent work. This second concept, which comes under the general category of "narrative point of view," was a central issue in literary—and particularly Formalist—studies in this period. The Formalists had been dealing with the issue since the latter part of the 1910s and had thus devised a number of terms for it: narrative "prism" and "refraction," for example. The Formalists' concern, along with their terminology, found its way into Vinogradov's work.[49]

It is not surprising that as Vinogradov's emphasis shifted

from the level of stylistics to that of poetics, the concept of "linguistic consciousness," which had served as a means of interpreting the semantic links between symbols, became directly associated with the issue of narration. "Linguistic consciousness" came to be seen by Vinogradov as a stylistically neutral baseline to which all other narrative voices stood in contrast.

One particular narrative issue that long drew the attention of the Formalists had been transplanted from Germany[50] to Russian soil by B. M. Eikenbaum in his work "How Gogol's 'The Overcoat' Is Made"; this was the problem of "skaz."

Skaz is a narrative device by which a narrator, who is sharply characterized by his substandard speech, which generally represents an identifiable ethnic, social, professional or age group, reproduces scenes and characterizes their participants in a mimicking fashion. The narrative, which has a live and ad-libbed character, usually gives the impression that it is directed towards the reader or some other audience.

In works narrated by this technique, there generally may be distinguished two levels of irony, one of which is felt in the attitude of the author toward his less sophisticated narrator, and the other of which is more pronounced and may be sensed in the attitude of the narrator toward the events and characters he portrays.

Vinogradov addressed the problem of skaz in most of his studies on Gogol and Dostoevsky and in other works as well. His concern with problems of skaz led him to develop his notion of "linguistic consciousness" in relation to it. By the time "Gogol and the Natural School" appeared, the concept had been modified and the term had been changed to "the authorial 'I'." In later works it became "the image of the author."[51]

Vinogradov developed this concept, not because he was interested in divining the psychology of the author, but because it was his view that:

> In the fabric of the words, in the devices of depiction [the artist's - D. E.] visage is perceived. But this is not the face of the "real," living Tolstoi,

Dostoevsky, or Gogol. It is the writer's "actor's" visage.[52]

This concept, which in Vinogradov's later work would be perceived as an important factor for distinguishing between various literary systems, was used more immediately in "Gogol and the Natural School" to establish a stylistic core to which all other stylistic streams might be compared. It should be noted that much of the time this notion of the stylistic core coincides with that of Gogol's aesthetic impulse or purpose. Thus, in identifying the styles which predominate in Gogol's work as a whole, or in individual texts, Vinogradov is seeking to single out those stylistic elements to which all other features in the work are subordinated.

V. V. Vinogradov's "Gogol and the Natural School"

In his work "Gogol and the Natural School," Vinogradov presents a critical survey of the most important theoretical works on Gogol developed in the first quarter of the century, and seeks to elaborate his own more comprehensive view of Gogol's poetics.

Having written continuously on the subject of Gogol for the three years preceding the publication of this article, Vinogradov is well-qualified for this task. In his "The Plot and Composition of Gogol's Tale 'The Nose' " ("Siuzhet i kompozitsiia povesti Gogolia 'Nos' ," 1921) he describes the "nosology" which had developed in Russia shortly after the published translation of Sterne's novel *The Life and Opinions of Tristram Shandy*. In a 1922 article, "An Experiment with a Linguistic Analysis of the Petersburg Poem 'The Double'," Vinogradov makes a comparative microanalysis of Gogol's "Notes of a Madman" ("Zapiski sumasshedshego,") and Dostoevsky's tale, pointing out the marked similarity of everything from the author's handling of time to their depiction of speech, narration, and movement. In an equally penetrating examination of the two authors, "The Plot and Composition of *Poor Folk*" ("Siuzhet i arkhitektonika romana Dostoevskogo *Bednye liudi*," 1924), he demonstrates how Dostoevsky's work represents the synthesis of Sentimentalism and Naturalism which Gogol had tried without success to effect. It is with such studies and Formalist theory as his background that Vinogradov initiates this survey and critique of early-20th century Gogol scholarship and sketches his own broad outline of Gogol's poetics.

True to the Formalist tradition, Vinogradov faults nearly every one of the works which he examines for its methodological electicism. Gippius is criticized for the mixing of biography and stylistics, Pereverzev is put to the task for his attempt to reduce *Dead Souls* to a document of Gogol's provincial social and economic environment, and others, Mandelshtam and Slonimsky, for example, are upbraided for using disparate means of categorizing stylistic elements. Those representing the Formalist School, Eikhenbaum and Tynianov, are criticized for their reductivist approach. But what troubles Vinogradov about each of the works he reviews is their failure to show the significance of the elements which they examine in broad perspective. On the basis of the studies he examines here, and on that of his own work of the preceding years, Vinogradov attempts to establish Gogol's aesthetic history—his poetics. This in essence entails an accounting of the stylistic, constructional and narrative diversity of Gogol's work. His most important accomplishments, in this respect, are in showing the influences present in Gogol's work at various points of time, and the relative significance of these influences; and in pointing out the motivations for the changes in Gogol's narrative technique.

In Vinogradov's view, a predilection for borrowing and an acute concern with style were the most characteristic features of Gogol the writer. Most of Gogol's literary career was marked by attempts to overcome or resurrect the latent sentimental element in his artistic consciousness by incorporating into his own work new popular material or treating old material in a new fashion.

Another peculiar feature of Gogol's style is his mixed linguistic core, which is composed of two distinct levels of language: archaic, Slavic, and bookish, and colloquial, everyday speech. Although this characteristic prevented him from using the Romantic style popular at that time, he managed to put it to his advantage.

Making use of his own mixed style, Gogol created tales with multiple stylistic levels on the model of Walter Scott's historical novels. He created the garrulous narrator, Rudy Panko, to serve as a device to unite the tales in a series, and developed still other narrative masks for each individual tale. Much of the verbal humor in these skaz-narrated works derived from the narrator's tendency to use language of a level beyond his own command. This particular technique, and that of allowing the skaz-narrator to mimickingly reproduce the clumsy phrases of the characters in the works, were among the most distinctive features of Gogol's works, according to Vinogradov.

Another aspect of Gogol's poetics which had its origins in these early works was its dramatic character. In *Evenings on a Farm near Dikanka* (*Vechera na khutore bliz Dikanki*, 1831-32) the skaz-narrators create the impression that they are directing a succession of stage scenes. The impression is enhanced by the fragmentary nature of the various scenes which makes them appear like short acts in a play.

According to Vinogradov, Gogol was quick to see that the Walter Scott style, which called for the depiction of characters of the lower spheres and the faithful description of their speech and milieu, provided him with the means to oppose the more lofty, idealized stylization of Sentimentalism.

But in the Frenetic style which superceded the Walter Scott tradition in the mid-30s, Gogol was to find the means to oppose Sentimentalism even more vigorously: the mechanical depiction of characters, the focus on the everyday, heightened corporeality, and pictures of horrors, torture and blood which was exemplified in the works of Jules Janin and Victor Hugo, stood in even sharper contrast to the idylls of Sentimentalism.

Gogol's fascination with the more violent branch of the Frenetic school, as expressed in Jules Janin's work, did not last long. He soon turned to Victor Hugo's grotesque version of horror, which involved the juxtaposition of the humorous and the horrible. This impulse was to be found in many of Gogol's works in the collections of tales which were published in 1835: *Mirgorod* (*Mirgorod*) and *Arabesques* (*Arabeski*).

In these tales as well as in those of the following year "The Nose" ("Nos") and "The Carriage" ("Kolyaska," 1836) Vinogradov observes a process of depsychologization of Gogol's narrators which he attributes to a general trend toward more objective narration.

But Vinogradov considers *The Inspector General* (*Revizor*, 1836) to represent a turning point in Gogol's career because it is only at this point that he frees himself from the influences of other writers and makes full use of the technique of naturalistic depiction which he has been developing throughout his career. The dramatic form enables him to rid himself of the narrators which he has been trying to conceal since 1835, and to achieve the narrative objectivity he had sought. It also provides him the chance to demonstrate more fully his capacity to create dialogue.

Because of a number of events surrounding the play, however, Gogol began to shift back towards Sentimentalism. This shift could be seen in two works which he published in 1842: *Dead Souls* (*Mertvye Dushi* and "The Overcoat" ("Shinel' "). Although Gogol did not return to the practice of using highly visible masks as he had done in his early works, a stream of sentimental lyricism is woven through these tales.

This sentimentalism is even more fully realized in Gogol's final work, *Selected Passages from a Correspondence with Friends* (*Vybrannye mesta iz perepiski s druziami,* 1846), where it is manifested in marked lyricism. The Naturalistic depictions which accompany it, however, do not complement it. Gogol found it difficult to maintain the objectivity required to support his Naturalistic tendencies. It was only for Gogol's successors, the Natural School, a group of followers he would not claim, to succeed in combining Naturalism with Sentimental pathos, and achieve an objective style of narration by doing away with the noisy chorus of narrators.

Debra K. Erickson

Notes

1. A. S. Bushmin, "O znachenii trudov akademika V. V. Vinogradova po literaturovedeniu," *Poetika i stilistika russkoi literatury* (Leningrad, 1971).
2. Ibid.
3. N. S. Pospelov, "Viktor Vladimirovich Vinogradov," *Sbornik statei po iazykoznaniiu* (Moscow, 1958), p. 16.
4. "V. V. Vinogradov" in *Great Soviet Encyclopedia* (New York, 1974), Vol. 5, pp. 480-481.
5. A. P. Chudakov. "Rannie raboty V. V. Vinogradova po poetike russkoi literatury," *Poetika russkoi literatury* (Moscow, 1976), p. 465.
6. *Great Soviet Encyclopedia*, Vol. 5, pp. 480-481.
7. Ibid.
8. Chudakov, p. 465.
9. Victor Erlich, *Russian Formalism: History, Doctrine* (The Hague, 1965), pp. 84-85.
10. Chudakov, p. 466.
11. Ibid.
12. Boris M. Eikhenbaum, "Teoriia formal'nogo metoda," *Literatura. Teoriia, kritika, polemika* (Leningrad, 1926), pp. 146-147.
13. Chudakov, p. 468.
14. Erlich, p. 85.
15. Eikhenbaum, p. 146.
16. See footnote in A. P. Chudakov's "V. V. Vinogradov: teoriia khudozhestvennoi rechi nachala XX veka," *O iazyke khudozhestvennoi prozy* (Moscow, 1980).
17. Erlich, p. 100.
18. Ibid., p. 148.
19. Ibid., p. 141.
20. Victor Erlich, *Twentieth-Century Russian Literary Criticism* (New Haven and London, 1975), p. 15.
21. Eikhenbaum, p. 121.
22. Erlich, *Russian Formalism*, pp. 172-173.
23. Ibid., p. 23.
24. Ibid., pp. 61-63.
25. Ibid., pp. 72-75.
26. Eikhenbaum, p. 122.
27. Erlich, *Russian Formalism*, pp. 76-77.
28. P. N. Medvedev, *Formal'nyi metod v literaturovedenii* (Leningrad, 1928), p. 224.
29. Erlich, *Russian Formalism*, p. 73.
30. Medvedev, p. 128.
31. Erlich, *Russian Formalism*, p. 76.

32. Ibid., pp. 75-76.
33. B. M. Eikhenbaum (1922) cited in *Russian Formalist Poetics in Translation*, vol. 4, p. 34.
34. Erlich, *Russian Formalism,* pp. 192-193.
35. Shklovskii (*Poetika,* 1919), p. 120, cited in Medvedev, p. 128.
36. Eikhenbaum, p. 127.
37. See "O teorii literaturnykh stilei" and "Iz stat'i k postroeniu teorii poeticheskogo iazyka," in *O iazyke khudozhestvennoi prozy* (Moscow, 1980).
38. See Vinogradov's review of Roman Iakobson's *Noveishaia russkaia poeziia* (Prague, 1921), pp. 463-464 in *Poetika russkoi literatury.*
39. V. V. Vinogradov, "O zadachakh stilistiki," *O iazyke khudozhestvennoi prozy* (Moscow, 1980), p. 6.
40. Ibid., p. 7.
41. Chudakov, p. 474.
42. Vinogradov, "O zadachakh stilistiki," p. 39.
43. Ibid., p. 5.
44. V. V. Vinogradov, "O teorii literaturnykh stilei." *O iazyke khudozhestvennoi prozy* (Moscow, 1980), p. 241.
45. Vinogradov, "O zadachakh stilistiki," p. 3.
46. Ibid.
47. A. P. Chudakov, "V. V. Vinogradov i teoriia khudozhestvennoi rechi nachala XX veka," *O iazyke khudozhestvennoi prozy* (Moscow, 1980), p. 292.
48. Vinogradov, "O zadachakh stilistiki," p. 39.
49. Chudakov, "V. V. Vinogradov i teoriia khudozhestvennoi rechi nachala XX veka," p. 310.
50. Ibid., p. 299.
51. Ibid., pp. 310-315.
52. Ibid., p. 311.

Bibliography

Chudakov, A. P. "Rannie raboty V. V. Vinogradova po poetike russkoi literary," *Poetika russkoi literatury*. Moscow: Nauka, 1976.

———. "V. V. Vinogradov i teoriia khudozhestvennoi rechi pervoi treti XX veka," *O iazyke khudozhestvennoi prozy*. Moscow: Nauka, 1980.

Eikhenbaum, Boris M. "Teoriia formal'nogo metoda," *Literatura. Teoriia, kritika, polemika*. Leningrad: Priboi, 1926.

Erlich, Victor. *Russian Formalism: History. Doctrine*. The Hague, The Netherlands: Mouton, 1965.

———. *Twentieth-Century Russian Literary Criticism*. New Haven and London: Yale University Press, 1975.

Medvedev, P. N. *Formal'nyi metod v literaturovedenii*. Leningrad: Priboi, 1928.

O'Toole, L. M. and Shukman, Ann. *Russian Poetics in Translation. Formalist Theory*. Vol. 4, 1976.

"Viktor Vladimirovich Vinogradov," in *The Great Soviet Encyclopedia*, Vol. 5, New York: Macmillan, 1974.

Vinogradov, V. V. "Etiudy o stile Gogolia," *Poetika russkoi literatury*. Moscow: Nauka, 1976.

———. "K morfologii natural'nogo stilia (Opyt lingvisticheskogo analiza peterburgskoi poemy *Dvoinik*)," in *Evoliutsiia russkogo naturalizma* in *Poetika russkoi literatury*. Moscow: Nauka, 1976.

———. "Naturalisticheskii grotesk (Siuzhet i kompozitsiia povesti Gogolia 'Nos')" in *Evoliutsiia russkogo naturalizma* in *Poetika russkoi literatury*. Moscow: Nauka, 1976.

———. "O teorii literaturnykh stilei," *O iazyke khudozhestvennoi prozy*. Moscow: Nauka, 1980.

———. "O zadachakh stilistiki. Nabliudeniia nad stilem Zhitiia protopopa Avvakuma," *O iazyke khudozhestvennoi prozy*. Moscow: Nauka, 1980.

———. "Romanticheskii naturalizm (Zhiul' Zhanin i Gogol')," *Poetika russkoi literatury*. Moscow: Nauka, 1976.

Part Two

Gogol and the Natural School

Chapter 1

The study of Gogol as a topic of literary history has scarcely begun. The topic involves a confusing tangle of ancillary problems. Some of these problems are of general theoretical literary interest and extend far beyond the bounds of Gogol's creative work. The cardinal questions of literary history (for example, the relationship between the Romantic and Realistic styles, the essence of Realism in Russian literature, and so on) were linked to the study of Gogol long ago, in the 1840s and 1850s (Belinsky, Chernyshevsky). This has disadvantaged the study of his poetics: his style has been branded with ill-defined terminological labels, forcing the mosaic complexity of its structure into the background. It is only since the beginning of this century that a path leading to the direct study of Gogol's style and poetics may be faintly discerned, albeit still of secondary import.

The clear stages of this path to the threefold study of Gogol's style, composition, and plot structure can be seen at a glance in a book by Professor Mandelshtam. His work is valuable in its selection of material and in its illumination of various problems (the role of foreign locutions in Gogol's style, the tendencies of his stylistic revisions, his use of repetitive formulae, and so on). Furthermore, he aids one in recognizing a certain core which is invariably present in Gogol's stylistic constructions, both in the speech of his characters and in the speech of his interpolated "skaz" narrators. Selections from Gogol's works are readily recognizable in this unique conglomeration of stylistic tendencies, regardless of whose speech is being reproduced—that of the narrator or that of the heroes.

The problem of the considerable similarity between narrative and conversational speech styles is of exceptional importance in the study of form in Gogol's work. Examination of this problem reveals those stylistic effects which are created by the constant "slipping" of the skaz from the imitation of the speech of the "author"—the outside observer—to the merging of his speech with that of the comic figures in the narrative. The narrator, an interpolated character (Medium) who weaves a verbal pattern, seems to shift back and forth between the author and the heroes in Gogol's works. As a result, in essence, it would be more appropriate to characterize the narrative style of Gogol's novellas as an orchestration of alternating voices, rather than as skaz (cf. the combining of various forms of speech which are not united by the image of a single narrator in "The Tale of How Ivan Ivanovich Quarrelled with Ivan Nikoforovich" and in "Nevsky Prospect").

Professor Mandelshtam provides rich material for the defining of this issue, but he does not pose the problem itself. On the contrary, he proposes a psychological explanation for these series of stylistic phenomena (pointing to Gogol's kinship with his heroes). Essentially, this is due to the fact that Professor Mandelshtam's book does not explore the compositional function of Gogol's stylistic devices. As a follower of Potebnia, he considered the problem on a psychological, rather than a "verbal," objective-stylistic plane (cf. Ovsianiko-Kulikovsky on the composition of *A Nest of Gentlefolk* and Rainov on *The Precipice*). Mandelshtam also leaves this question aside in his work on the "artistic word." But henceforth in his work one finds only an external, morphological description of devices, rather than a definition of their functions in various artistic constructions.

That is one side of the coin. On the other side one finds that the dynamics of Gogol's style are not reproduced or explained. On the contrary, the abstracted devices are lined up in a single column after being extracted from the works of various periods. Moreover, it happens that in one stylistic variant, a well-known device (for example, the piling-up of proper names with no explanation of their concrete meaning) is viewed as a compositional peak (the style of Rudy Panko); in another variant it is regarded as a chance survivor with a sharply changed function (in *Dead Souls*).

Eliminating thus the problem of composition, Professor Mandelshtam was obliged to forgo differentiating between the forms of style as well as describing the changes and alternations of various stylistic systems which occur in Gogol's poetics. For Mandelshtam, Gogol's works of various periods appeared to spread over a single chronological plane. Indeed, he examines Gogol's work from a static perspective as a single, integral "flowerbed" from which he has weeded out "that period lacking in any style." However, there also are allusions to the genesis of individual devices and to the variability of basic stylistic tendencies (the evolution of a comic effect, the role of neologisms in various epochs, and so forth).

At this point, a new tangle of methodological contradictions arises. Professor Mandelshtam has combined two disparate methodological principles: at times, in drawing morphological comparisons, he examines Gogol's stylistic forms as an objective given, existing beyond the sphere of Gogol's poetic consciousness; at other times as an immanent awareness shaped by the writer's aesthetic experience.

The first method naturally inclines toward historical investigation, toward the literary traditions involved, the motives underlying their selection by the artist, as well as his synthesizing devices. Mandelshtam's remarks about traditional images in Gogol, about the poetic folk elements, stylistic formulae and devices from Pushkin, Zhukovsky and Krylov reflected in Gogol's works, rest upon this method. Yet these features are incidental. Mandelshtam does not point out the basic traditions interwoven in Gogol's style.

The second method directs the scholar along the path of psychological interpretation of stylistic phenomena. Potebnia preceded Mandelshtam in this respect. All the same, the principles of psycho-aesthetic and psycho-biographical explanations are combined on this plane as well: the physiology of Gogol's daily life is insinuated into his aesthetics (cf. especially the chapters on Gogol's style in relation to his personality and on the similarities of his own language to that of the characters in his works.)

Thus, Professor Mandelshtam's book on the character of Gogol's style affords a rich collection of stylistic phenomena grouped together under the general rubrics: "Gogolian epithets," "similes," "the Ukrainian element," "humor," "epic character," and so forth. The organizing principles behind these groupings are contradictory and often lie beyond the sphere of linguistics and literature. They reveal neither the evolution of Gogol's stylistic forms, nor the organic unity of his style as a reflection of his own poetic consciousness.[1] Problems of the poetics of individual works are left untouched. However, this book is the starting point for the majority of subsequent works on Gogol's poetics, particularly those which approach his style as systems of aesthetically shaped verbal phenomena. For this reason it was necessary to mention it prior to surveying the newest works on Gogol's stylistics. For the most part these works revolve around the material excerpted by Mandelshtam, but they give it a different stylistic interpretation.

The general direction in this new treatment of the features of Gogol's style was sketched by V. V. Rozanov in his articles on Gogol (" 'The Legend of the Grand Inquisitor' by F. M. Dostoevsky. With two appended studies on Gogol"). Rozanov, defining Gogol as a depictor of "subjects and phenomena at their limits rather than in their actual existence,"[2] regards his work as an interlacing of two forms of style, two artistic principles: "the traits of one go endlessly higher, whereas those of the other go downward; both *distance themselves from reality* and are equally *devoid* of movement, *life*, and spirituality." The combination of a "constant lyricism" and the "dead fabric" of a Naturalistic "wax language" is the essence of Gogol's style. Rozanov considers the "marionettish deathlike character of Gogol's types, contrastively heightened by the dynamism of the material world," as a correlative of Gogol's "mosaic of words." Gogol's types are "minute wax figures, yet they grimace so skillfully that we long have suspected them of movement." Likewise Rozanov, focusing on Gogol's devices of depiction, characterizes his method as the "painting" of types, as the "selective blending of other similar, continuous and reinforcing traits into one chosen thematic trait in the created image."[3]

In this manner, Rozanov, without a large arsenal of scientifically selected facts yet with a striking feel for language, noted the most essential characteristics of Gogol's style; they now required only further linguistic description and precise formulation: (1) its grotesque character, consisting of interruptive comic narrative speech, "a stream of mockery," of strained, "pitiful" declamation; (2) the static, deathlike "wax" Symbolism of the portrait, overemphasizing a single trait; (3) motor images in the description of *nature morte* and things in general.

In establishing the forms of Gogol's style, Rozanov subjected them to a psychological, artistic interpretation and was prepared to make the contrast between the "disparagement of man" and "constant lyricism" in Gogol's work the basis of a "history" of the great man's "soul." Thus the dualism characteristic of Mandelshtam arises in Rozanov's work as well: the objective description of stylistic phenomena is ascribed "philosophically" to corresponding psychological peculiarities in the personality of the writer.

It is natural to conclude that Rozanov's successors in both the description and study of Gogol's style follow two basic avenues. Some either reduce the distinguishing features of his artistic work to the peculiarities of Gogol's own psyche, or contemplate them in parallel; others pursue a schematically projected description of stylistic forms in the manner outlined by Rozanov. It must be noted that the tendency to combine matters of style with the psychological issue of Gogol's inner world emerges organically from the earlier psycho-biographical and socio-psychological traditions in the study of Gogol. Even those literary historians who continue to occupy the armchairs of publicists, now, at the beginning of the twentieth century, in the epoch of Symbolism, contrast Gogol the irrealist, who knew nothing of reality but who, of course, was by nature a civic writer, with the Gogol of the 19th century, a realist copying reality (Vengerov). Others, disposed toward the psychology of artistic creation, term him an artist-experimenter (Ovsianiko-Kulikovsky).

And now the works of his associates—those forerunners and contemporaries who treated a similar range of themes—are being substituted for that life which earlier everyone fondly alluded to as the source of Gogol's creative art (Kotliarevsky). In a word, the reaction against the view which saw Gogol as a "realist," a reaction based upon biographical, psychological and literary data, dates from the onset of the present century.

One line of Gogol scholars, those who represent the study of stylistics and the aesthetics of verbal art and verge upon this reaction, submit to the reigning psychologism. These are the scholars from the camp of the Symbolists: Valery Briusov, Andrei Belyi and Innokenty Annensky. They seek to intensify the general notion of Gogol as a hyperbolist reduced to ashes, an irrealist Symbolist, and an Impressionist. In his speech, "Reduced to Ashes," Valery Briusov, proceeding from Rozanov's formula (on Gogol's contemplation of phenomena and objects at their limits), demonstrates that Gogol was guided by the principle of hyperbole in forming verbal material (Potebnia and later Mandelshtam had spoken brilliantly about this). Briusov, however, is not engaged so much by the stylistic analysis of hyperbole in Gogol's works as he is by the demonstration of the irreality, the improbability of Gogol's artistically created world, which he links to a tendency toward extremes, toward exaggeration, characteristic of Gogol's psyche.

In his article "Gogol,"[4] Andrei Belyi, on the one hand, develops Rozanov's ideas with a bent in the direction of Symbolist poetics. He writes that in Gogol's work the earth is "not the earth," and that two worlds reside in it: "the superhuman," "garbed in a romantic veil of the sun's rays," woven of syncretic, unreal images, "where colors, aromas and sounds intermingle," and the "pre-human world" of "beasts" and "radishes," constructed from animal and material symbolism. On the other hand, switching to the verbal technique, he maintains that "the fabric of Gogolian speech is a series of technical tricks," and provides a schematic description of certain of them. For the most part he adheres to Mandelshtam's ideas, but he adds some of his own valuable observations on euphonic phenomena and rhythmic-syntactic figures in Gogol's style. Belyi includes a psychological-metaphysical interpretation of Gogol's personality and creative work in conjunction with this analysis of artistic forms.

After presenting a general psychological profile of Gogol in the article "The Aesthetics of *Dead Souls*,"[5] in which he dwells upon Gogol's "typical corporeality, which oppressed and crushed the world" (cf. Rozanov's character profile of Gogol), Innokenty Annensky offers some particularly brilliant observations on how the categories of the animate and personal and the inanimate are merged in Gogol's poetics. For instance, on the depiction of Sobakevich he writes: "The muzhiks, the huts, even the *names of the muzhiks*, the food, the chairs, the thrush, the tail-coat, and the heroes on the walls—all were Sobakeviches. Yet, while making everything into himself, this central Sobakevich fatally sank to the level of things, in the last analysis his very typicality becoming little more than a nightmarish caricature." Then in bold brushstrokes, Annensky outlines a general definition of "the style of the portrait" in Gogol, characterizing it as a method of personifying external and material details: "And Manilov? Isn't he really all lips in a juicy smacking kiss? And those people—eyebrows? even people—smells... And yet isn't there something else, either in the Procurator or Petrushka, besides the eyebrows and smells so wondrously and monstrously personified?"[6]

With regard to these stylistic phenomena, Gogol's artistic task is depicted as the establishment of a system of material images and metaphors, as the immersion of the Pushkinian word into a "fathomless corporeality."

Concerning the other features of Gogol's style, Annensky stresses his Impressionistic tendencies ("Gogol wrote in patches of color and form"), the syncretism of his images, and his "oratorical element."

Thus the scholar-artists from the camp of the Symbolists, struggling with the naively realistic attitude of the literary historical tradition preceding Gogol's Naturalism, illuminate Gogol's artistic forms from a psychoaesthetic point of view (particularly those artists who are close to the poetics of symbolism). They do not approach Gogol's style as a historical phenomenon—as an assembly of elements formed by literary styles and as a starting point in the development of subsequent styles—and they do not delve into individual aspects of Gogol's poetics. Foremost for them are Gogol's spiritual personality and a general, intuitive psychological interpretation of Gogol's dominant stylistic tendencies.[7]

A ripening interest in problems of artistic form demanded the continued study of style. Moreover, the reaction against psychologism, reflected so sharply in the literature and poetics of Futurism, naturally suggested a shift in matters of Gogolian style to a plane projected beyond the bounds of Gogol's own consciousness, a focus on the study of Gogol's "word per se," on words as objects. This new stage in the study of Gogolian style began in the years of the war and revolution. Two lines may be distinguished in it. Arrayed along one line are those scholars who seek to introduce a sociological basis to an understanding of the artistic forms borne beyond the sphere of Gogol's consciousness. They operate by two different methods which, as a result of artificial interbreeding, now have been united under the name of the formal-sociological method. V. F. Pereverzev's book, *The Work of Gogol* (1914), lies at the onset of this line. Since this work and others connected with it transfer the center of attention from problems of style to questions of plot structure in the broad sense of the term (inclusive of thematics), and in part to composition, it would be more convenient to discuss them in a separate chapter.[8]

For the time being we will focus upon those studies of Gogol which are of a purely formal character, without any sociological superstructures. Most of them only peripherally touch upon Gogol's style, using it as material for general theoretical discussions. B. M. Eikhenbaum's essay: "How Gogol's 'The Overcoat' Is Made" (cf. *Poetika,* 1919) should be placed foremost among these articles. In this piece, the artistic work is viewed as a given—imposed from without upon the poet's consciousness, an "artificial" construction, reflecting not the visage of the artist, but solely the devices of his creation. In applying this general principle to Gogol's "Overcoat" Eikhenbaum is following, on the one hand, the traditions of the Gogol scholars who derive from Rozanov's work: "Gogol's characters are all petrified poses." "The real dynamics and thereby even the composition of his things lie in the structuring of the skaz, in verbal play." But these ideas are made more complex by the problem of skaz.

The problem of skaz is linked to the study of the functions of those interpolated figures, narrators, to whom the author resorts in organizing various forms of style. Käte Friedmann's book *Die Rolle des Erzählers in der Epik* (Leipzig, 1910) is devoted to this question. To a certain extent, it is under her influence that Eikhenbaum distinguishes between the adventure novella, in which plot predominates, and the skaz novella, in which the personal tone of the author is the principal component. Within the bounds of the latter, there are two types—narrative (epic) and representational (dramatic). Eikhenbaum includes among the material for the analysis of the representational skaz those of Gogol's novellas in which may be noted the tendency "not merely to narrate, not merely to speak, but to represent mimetically and articulately."

Thus, the basic task in the study of Gogol's style is presumed to lie in the analysis of his skaz forms. A penchant for the works on the methodology of speech by representatives of the school of "Ohrenphilologie," Professors Sievers, Saran and others, is reflected in this issue (especially when Eikhenbaum focuses attention upon the tone of the narrator and the changing of intonation).

One also senses a refracting of the perception of Gogolian skaz through the prism of the problems of storytelling facing contemporary Russian belletrists—Remizov, Belyi, Zamiatin, and others. With regard to the definition of Gogolian skaz as "representational," Eikhenbaum characterizes Gogol's style as an organization of words and sentences based mainly "on the principle of expressive speech, in which a special role belongs to articulation, mimicry, sound gestures, and the like." Characteristic of such a style is the overshadowing of the semantics of words by their "sound semantics": "articulation and its acoustic effects are foregrounded as an expressive device" (cf. the role of first names and surnames). Pathetic declamation exists alongside comic skaz in Gogol's novellas.

In Eikhenbaum's opinion, two main devices in Gogol's own reading, as is testified to by his listeners, correspond to these two forms of style which were sharply delineated by Rozanov in his analysis of "The Overcoat." Thus, a unique focusing of attention upon skaz, upon language play, is basic to this train of thought. This represents a return (and a fruitful one at that) to the perception of Gogol's contemporaries. In analyzing comic skaz Eikhenbaum focuses his attention upon intonation as a syntactical organizing factor, upon the contrast between the syntactical structuring of speech and its lexical embodiment, upon the changing of tonalities, and only slightly on the properties of Gogolian semantics. Eikhenbaum singles out puns, the device of the acoustic effect of "trans-sense" words, and the comic use of foreign locutions, i.e., those things which already had been noted in Mandelshtam's book.

Truly new for these years, and natural as an outgrowth of Futurism, was the attempt to free the analysis of speech from the set toward a system of semantic shifts which create an individual poetic language, and the foregrounding of "articulation and acoustics." Correspondingly, Gogol's style in "The Overcoat" is regarded only as "a kind of system of sound gestures," as "a kind of mimetically articulated sound series." Yet everyone understands, of course, that a system of semantic correspondences is found in "expressive speech" (even if it is called "mimetically articulated voiced speech"). This system of sense correspondences, and the symbols of which it consists, may be complicated and transformed by various means of voiced and mimetic expression, but it is not swallowed up or destroyed by them.

Eikhenbaum, leaving semantics aside, limits himself to indicating a change in the tonal coloration of speech in the style of "The Overcoat." He singles out such forms as "careless, naive banter, familiar loquacity." "businesslike epic skaz," "sentimental-melodramatic declamation," tracing their interweaving in the composition of "The Overcoat" and characterizing their conjoining as grotesque.

It should be noted, however, that Eikhenbaum's interpretation of the artistic conception of "The Overcoat" as a grotesque "game" of words is purely intuitive, results from his "critical sense" and the general premises of Futurist aesthetics, and lies outside the framework of the historical tradition of the "civil servant" tales of that epoch. For this reason, his suggested reading of "The Overcoat" is one-sided and distorted.

Thus, in characterizing Gogol's style as "representational" skaz and decisively isolating the narrator-performer (who almost becomes a comedian playing with artistic devices) from the author's spiritual experience, Eikhenbaum transfers Rozanov's basic points to the plane of an objective analysis of the structure of Gogolian speech (mainly from a phonetic-syntactic standpoint). What Eikhenbaum wishes to suggest with his selection of quotes from contemporaries on Gogol's manner of reading, however, is not clearly stated. Is there not concealed here the very same empirical basis for "representational skaz" in Gogol, namely in the suggestion that it belongs to a certain type of inner discourse?

Closely linked to Eikhenbaum's article are the remarks on Gogol's style found in Iu. N. Tynianov's brochure: *Dostoevsky and Gogol (Toward a Theory of Parody)* (1921). In the author's opinion, Gogol's main device in character description is "the device of the mask." The very notion of the mask, however, remains incompletely defined. It is related to Rozanov's idea of "little wax figures," but sometimes is synonymous with the designation "type" in the traditional sense (p. 15). A new concept of the "verbal mask" (and, by the way, of names) is introduced in connection with Eikhenbaum's observation on "sound semantics."

Another of Gogol's stylistic devices on which Tynianov dwells is the device of material metaphors. In his view, the basis of Gogol's humor is "the discrepancy between his animate and material images." "Gogol's main device is a system of material metaphors, masks having identical application on both of his planes (high and low)" (cf. in this regard certain of Innokenty Annensky's observations, see above, p. 37).

Given the pre-eminence of this approach to the artistic

work as an aggregate of devices, as an unadorned verbal fabric which, at times, is not even draped over any subject (cf. Annensky, pp. 17-18), it is curious to note in a few instances the imputation of features of style to the psychology and personality of the artist ("Gogol saw things in an extraordinary fashion"). A particularly pointed mingling of stylistic and psychological levels is revealed in the second part of Tynianov's book, where it is demonstrated that Foma Opiskin in Dostoevsky's novel *The Village of Stepanchikovo and Its Inhabitants* is a parodic figure: "Gogol's personality provided material for the parody; Foma's speeches parody Gogol's correspondence with his friends." Yet from the author's comparisons it is quite clear that there is no stylistic, that is verbal, parody of the devices of speech organization from *Correspondence* in *The Village of Stepanchikovo*. The thematic coincidences and similarity of individual phrases in Foma's speech and in the *Correspondence with Friends* attests only to the use of the *Correspondence* as material for the creation of "a typical character." And if one speaks about parody, then one must see it not in a system of verbal displacements, but in a correspondence between themes and phrases from Gogol's *Correspondence* and the hero with negative psychological characteristics.

I. Gruzdev's article "Character and Mask" in the Berlin almanac *The Serapion Brothers* (1922) is even more closely related to Eikhenbaum's article on "The Overcoat." Gruzdev, discussing the role of the narrator in the construction of the novella and novel, with a reference to Eikhenbaum (p. 221), tries to take the last step on the path towards the depsychologization of art and asserts: "the artist is always a mask." Using illustrations from Gogol's "Nevsky Prospect," he schematically demonstrates the switching of "grotesque" and "fantastic masks." Thus, even here novelty lies only in the terminology (a new sense of the word "mask").

If the enumerated works of the "formal" type comprise one group, then A. L. Slonimsky's book: *The Technique of the Comic in Gogol (Tekhnika komicheskogo u Gogolia)* (in the series *Voprosy poetiki,* Prague, 1923) must be viewed in isolation. It is true that the general principles of this study are closely related to the formal tradition in the study of Gogol, i.e., the works by Mandelshtam, Eikhenbaum, and others, but they are made more complex by the influence on the author of psychological aesthetics (especially in the persons of Lipps and Volkelt). In this respect, Slonimsky's book falls into two parts. In one part, a definition of humor and the comic grotesque is given (according to Lipps and Volkelt). Also presented here are, with illustrations from *The Inspector General,* "The Tale of Two Ivans," and "The Overcoat," the characteristics of those devices whereby the fusion of the comic and serious (crucial to humor) is affected in Gogol's work. In Gogol's work the combining of the comic and the serious is realized in the form of unexpected transitions: from forced, elevated pathos to abrupt comic denouements. The abruptness of these contrasts in conjunction with the distorted comic images comprises, in Slonimsky's opinion, the essence of the comic grotesque. This comic grotesque reaches its fullest expression in "The Overcoat" and *Dead Souls*.

After 1842, while working on the second volume of *Dead Souls*, the element of the grotesque is diminished, due to a strengthening of the elements of pathos and didacticism.

The grotesque sharpness of the comic effect is bound up with the general implausibility, the simplified motivation, and a certain arbitrariness in the linking of events. Because of this, Gogol's creative work does not fit into the ready formulas of "Realism."

In the second chapter, investigating the technique of "comic alogism," a device noted by Mandelshtam, Slonimsky operates exclusively in the sphere of problems related to the forms of this device. However, this operation takes place along two axes. In one, the fabric of speech is investigated objectively- as the displacement of a semantic series during the construction of the phrase ("the humor of incommensurabilities"), when a rejoinder interrupts a dialogue ("a conversation between deaf characters"), and punning rejoinders result in misunderstandings ("the humor of logical stasis"). In another chapter he establishes general psychological categories ("the humor of whimsical associations"), wherein heterogeneous phenomena are introduced as of a literary order, i.e., from an objective stylistic point of view, such as the logically unmotivated linkings of phrases placed side by side in Chmykhov's letter in *The Inspector General*, in Poprishchin's speech, and in Khlestakov's conversation with Rastakovsky. Thus, Slonimsky blends two non-combinable methods of classifying devices: on general psychological grounds, and on the basis of semantic uniformity.

Slonimsky also adds a survey of his compositional reflections to the analysis of stylistic expressions of "comic alogism." He sees them in the non-motivation of comical processes in Gogol's works, in the lack of "natural positive motivation," and in the destruction of logical and causal connections between those phenomena which form the "strange" world of Gogol's art.

Surveying this entire chain of works on the study of Gogol's style, it is easy to detect in them one common trait: they do not engage the problem of the genesis of Gogol's style, its sources in literary traditions. They only describe the forms of Gogol's style, either in an aspect of the psychology of an individual work, or as general problems in the theory of literature. Only certain of Mandelshtam's remarks and, if you will, those of Vasily Gippius serve as exceptions. Incidentally, in the latter's work one encounters only a posing of problems emanating from the research of predecessors.

Chapter 2

Most of the studies on Gogol's artistic forms are concentrated in the realm of style; one can easily outline the general stages of the formal, aesthetic interpretation of Gogol over the last quarter of a century on the basis of these works. Some of these articles naturally connect problems of style with those of composition (for example, the works of A. Slonimsky, B. Eikhenbaum), yet in a narrow sense: either with the aim of finding one general formula for Gogol's composition, or to point out general tendencies in the replacement of forms of speech with varying tonality. There are no special works on Gogol's poetics devoted to problems of composition in specific works, or to general principles of composition (unless one includes my article: "The Plot and Composition of Gogol's Tale: 'The Nose' "). Of course, these issues are quite broadly discussed in two books: *The Work of Gogol* (1914) by V. F. Pereverzev, and *Gogol* by Vasily Gippius (1924). (I shall not speak about Professor Ivan Ermakov's book *Sketches on the Psychology of Gogol's Work* because I lack a sense of humor.) But the way in which these scholars raise these issues is so closely related to their general methodology and the conception of Gogol's work upon which it is based, that it is more expedient to examine these works in all their parts and in all their methodological distinctiveness.

Turning away from these books for a moment, we see that there remains the one general problem of composition in Gogol's poetics which has been brought to the fore by recent literary quests: the problem of the link between Gogol's composition and the poetics of "Sternianism." The mosaic pasting of fragments, the characteristic principle of Gogol's composition, the abruptness of digressions serving a whimsical playing with plot, the lack of logical motivation, or playing with motivation, the precipitous descent of the compositional line into infinity (as in the tale about "Shponka" and partly in "The Nose")—various scholars have posed all these devices as dependent upon the "Sternian" tradition: drawn directly from Sterne or from his Russian epigones.[9] Such, so to speak, is the general achievement of the epoch.

Individual solutions to the compositional problems in Gogol's poetics may be easily singled out in a survey of the general studies on Gogol's creative work, i.e., Pereverzev and Gippius. V. F. Pereverzev's book *The Work of Gogol*, in describing Gogol's works as an "objective reality" consisting of "objective elements of style" and of "objectively presented images," seeks to interpret them sociologically as a "vivid aesthetic embodiment of the life of a certain social milieu." The author singles out two elements in Gogol's art—Cossack and small landholding elements—which were fantastically interwoven in *Evenings*, but subsequently isolated from one another, and decisively so after 1834. Pereverzev seeks to explain the forms of style on the basis of the distinguishing features of these two elements.

Pereverzev likewise deduces in similar fashion the disjointed composition of Gogol's works from the properties of the naturalistically depicted landowner-serf way of life. Turning to Gogol's landscape, Pereverzev seeks to demonstrate that its poverty is conditioned, on the one hand, by the poverty of nature surrounding the petty-landowner's estate and the town, and, on the other hand, by the absence of genuine contact between this impoverished world of nature and the world of "stout, immobile bodies rooted in the petty estate." The immobility of the petty-landholding serf system especially lends itself to portrait painting. Such is the source of Gogol's vivid portraits, which are based on the depiction of purely external features, sometimes even on a single item of dress. Their extraordinary simplicity and primitiveness is their distinguishing feature. Therefore, notwithstanding their variety, Gogol's types are easily classified since they are the product of a single milieu and possess the same generic traits, among which the most basic is "smug idleness."

Gogol's idlers may be broken down into three ranks. The *sensitive* ones: Shponka, Pererepenko, Afanasy Ivanovich Tovstogub, and Manilov. Representative of city life are Podkolesin, Tentetnikov (a variant of this type from the large estate milieu), while Bashmachkin and Piskarev represent variants of the urban bourgeoisie. Then there are the "active idlers": Chertokutsky, Nozdrev, and Khlestakov—"as characters, Nozdrev and Khlestakov are one and the same, only in different uniforms"; Koshkarev from the large estate milieu; and Chertkov and Poprishchin from the milieu of the urban bourgeoisie. Finally, there are the sober-minded characters: Storchenko, Sobakevich, Pliushkin, and Skvoznik-Dmukhanovsky; and Kostanzhoglo from the large landholding milieu. Together with these "monotone" characters "woven from a single element," Pereverzev also finds in Gogol's work complex idlers who combine features of the simple idlers. They are created by combining the characteristics of the Manilovs, the Nozdrevs, and the Sobakeviches in one image, each time in varying proportions.

Gogol's inclination to leave the familiar, small-estate plots and characters for the world of fantastic reveries about Little-Russian Cossack life stemmed from the psychological anguish and disenchantment which arose among the best representatives of the landed class in the epoch of the decline of the landed-patriarchal social order under the influence of the monetary-exchange culture.

The sociological interpretation of the artistic work in Pereverzev's book is interesting. Not all literary historians (among those who employ such a method) agree with Pereverzev's explanations. A. Tseitlin[10] has shown that his deducing the features of Gogolian composition from the fragmentation of the petty-landholding order is unconvincing (cf. *The Tales of Belkin*).

Works are already appearing, however, in which Pereverzev's general principles serve as a background for illuminating particular issues in Gogol's work. Such is an article by V. V.

Danilov, "Gogol's *Dead Souls* as a Chronicle of Russian Life of the 20s," in which the author, on the basis of a random selection of factual material from *Dead Souls*,[11] a premeditated shuffling of negligible details, and a complete disregard of contrary indications, demonstrates that the first part of *Dead Souls* reflects the economic side of life in the 1820s, and that the second part reflects the 1830s.

Pereverzev himself, however, rather than raising a sociological superstructure over the artistic system of Gogol's work, undertook a "reduction" of Gogolian poetics in order to place it on a narrow sociological base. He employs this "reduction" so as to eliminate the basic devices of Gogol's work (for example, in the structuring of "The Overcoat," *Dead Souls, The Inspector General*, and so forth). Under this method of addressing artistic material, however, the entire formal aesthetic part of analysis turns out to be only mechanically appended to the sociological discussion.

One has only to move beyond the bounds of Gogol's work to his literary forerunners and his literary milieu to discern the real sources of his devices, and to be convinced of their freedom from any "petty landholding" affiliation. Otherwise it would be necessary to enroll among the petty landholders of pre-reform Russia, for example, Walter Scott, Hoffmann, Tieck, Sterne, Jules Janin, Victor Hugo, all their Russian epigones, and likewise, incidentally—the anonymous authors of Nativity plays (*vertepy*) and interludes and many other of Gogol's forerunners. Pereverzev feels liberated only when he parts with Gogol's works and adapts the heroes' names to a description of possible psychological stratifications in the milieu of the petty-landholding gentry.

The failure of Pereverzev's socio-formal observations on Gogol's work results not only from an insufficient preliminary analysis of the formal aesthetic problems of Gogol's style, as Tseitlin thinks, but also from the root antinomy of literary-historical and sociological interpretations of artistic material.

Gippius's book, *Gogol*, poses as its basic task the summarizing of the achievements of the "Gogolists," but does not confine itself to this. The author's intention is "to add certain forgotten data to what has been achieved earlier and independently to raise certain viewpoints."

What is new in Gippius's outline of "Gogol's personal and creative development" comprises a few lines in the general schema in which the author sketches Gogol's creative path, and his study of particular problems in Gogol's work. His method is psycho-aesthetic. Gippius poses the problems of Gogol as the bearer of a specific aesthetic consciousness, the evolution of this consciousness under the impact of various literary influences, the embodiment of its principles in Gogol's artistic work, and a definition of the literary traditions in those genres and forms of style in which Gogol wrote. Gogol's personal path is seen by Gippius as just such a schematic pattern: the youthful, individual mission which inheres in his work from the onset becomes complicated by aesthetic considerations ("Gans Kiukhelgarten"), and is shunted aside by that aestheticism which is the basic element of Gogol's psyche in the 30s.

Gogol's aesthetic individualism, which, after *The Inspector General*, had just begun to be associated with a mystic sense of mission, flourishes anew in Italy, his second homeland. His new aesthetic manifestos appear: "Rome" and "The Portrait" (in the second edition).

Symptoms of a decisive turn toward moralism in Gogol's creative work manifest themselves in the composition of "The Overcoat" ("the pathetic passage"), in the reworking of *Taras Bulba*, and in *Leaving the Theater*. In *Dead Souls*, too, there sounds the pathos of a personal superiority over the philistines, a pathos which in the process of work was transformed from an aesthetic individualism into moralism. However, the denunciatory impulse linked to this pathos did not take the form of a social protest: it was directed against each individual philistine, and not against the social order.

From moralism Gogol's path turned towards religion; yet his path consisted of twists and turns and was by no means direct. The result of this spiritual quest was an idyll: *Selected Passages from a Correspondence with Friends,* in which Gogol depicts "the idyllic domestic, social and political life of morally transformed people." This is a peculiar social "utopia," a "reactionary social mixture" with a religious lining. But the book was a failure, and in the ensuing years—after a useless pilgrimage—Gogol no longer dreams of "higher levels," but strives for a rebirth in work. He becomes a "day-laborer." Furthermore, his ideology changes imperceptibly. "The former ideal was the transformation of the existing forms of domestic, landowning, and government orders, which nevertheless was grounded in an involuntary idealization and which now was being replaced by an ascetic ideal of renunciation." One may note in Gogol's work a turning from Romantic realism to Naturalism, from hyperbolic caricature to "mathematical fidelity to reality," from subjectivism to "objectivism." The gathering of information about life and people, dry "statistics" on Russia, works of the "Natural School" which derived from Gogol but then moved away from him—all this provided everyday and psychological material for the Naturalistic reproduction of the world in art. The failure of *Correspondence* led Gogol to a renunciation of "the ideal." In this regard the construction of the "poem"—its plan, material, and artistic devices—changed decisively. Physiologism was replaced by psychologism, and the second part of *Dead Souls* was transformed into a Realistic psychological novel, in which, however, resound echoes of the "third idyll" (that is, *Correspondence*) in the images of Kostanzhoglo, Murazov, and the governor-general.

Thus does Gippius depict the schema of Gogol's personal and creative development. The schema is not new. Its basic lines were noted earlier, by Kotliarevsky, Shenrok, Lukoianovsky, Zenkovsky, Bogomolov, and others. But they traced the schema in an excessively rectilinear fashion. Gippius then complicated it, attempting to reflect in it psychological nuances and vacillations. Gogol's evolving aesthetic views were inserted into the schema and organically linked to its other parts with particular success.

It is true that Gippius's dependence on V. V. Zenkovsky's work, "Gogol in His Religious Quests,"[12] is especially noticeable here. Zenkovsky, however, in examining Gogol's aesthetic and moral quests as the manifestation of a single mystical impulse, traces their *parallel* reflections in his work, proceeding from the supposition that Gogol objectified in images the movement "of his own soul." Zenkovsky sees the primordial tendency of Gogol's psyche in his moralism, a tendency which collided with his aesthetic emotions but was not veiled by them. The very humor of Gogol's works in the period after *Evenings* leads him to conclude that Gogol's attitudes toward people were twofold, characterized "by a moral striving to serve them," and an aesthetic rejection of them. Thus, the schema of Gogol's development is "straightened out" by Zenkovsky. And the great artist's religious mysticism turns out to be seemingly a direct result of the moral aesthetic quests of youth, which then summoned a general turn toward emotional experience and, in turn, marked the genuine mystic in Gogol.

It is impossible to deny that Zenkovsky's work provides a profound psychological and philosophical analysis of the general cast of Gogol's emotional thought, and of his aesthetic, moral and religious experiences and convictions. Yet all Zenkovsky's observations are incompatible with a genuine literary-historical study of Gogol's works, and are tied to the general movement of Russian religious and philosophical thought. While Zenkovsky's characterization of the aesthetic and religio-moral base in Gogol's work is extremely valuable for the literary historian, nonetheless it will require several literary-historical corrections on his part.

Gippius has provided just these corrections. The result is that in his book Gogol's personal and artistic histories have been interwoven; Gogol's works are linked to his spiritual world. One may argue against this method of literary study, but one cannot deny that it led Gippius to an integral view of Gogol's work, although he was influenced to a considerable degree by Zenkovsky's article.

Even if one distances oneself from this psychological canvas on which the author occasionally did not wholly consistently sketch objective formal patterns, there remains in Gippius's work a series of new solutions or new perceptions of particular problems in Gogol's poetics.

1. Gippius has pointed out parallel plots to "Diary of a Madman" which were part of the preceding literary tradition (the short story about the French officer who fancies himself

the King of Spain, "The Mad Gloryseeker," which appeared in the *Moscow Telegraph* in 1826, and a few others (cf. the journal *Butterfly*, 1829, No. 34).

2. The demonstrations of a link between the preceding vaudevillian tradition and the generally comedic plots of *The Inspector General* and *The Marriage* are extremely interesting. The full scope of Gippius's independent findings can not be fully presented here, but it is evident partly in his laconic observations, and partly in his notes. He traces these plots to similar situations in the comedies of the eighteenth century (works by Fonvizin, Kapnist, Kniazhnin, and others), and in vaudevilles of the first third of the nineteenth century (Khmelnitsky, Pisarev, Lensky, and others). He also gives some general indications of ties to the Molierian tradition and sketches in broad strokes the general literary background of comic dramaturgy prior to Gogol.

3. Deserving of attention is the mention made in passing to Fielding's influence on Gogol's poetics. One might adduce many examples of this made during Gogol's lifetime.

4. Gippius's observations on the composition of the poema *Dead Souls* are valuable. His division of the first volume of *Dead Souls* into two parts, and the discussion of static portrait depictions in the first, and, in the second, the dynamics of the adventure parody and the classification of "passions" and "circles" according to which Gogol's heroes are placed are brilliant, even though they are based on certain hints by predecessors.

5. There remains a strong sense that *Correspondence with Friends* is an idyll with the character of a utopia, that this purely literary composition is organically linked to Sentimental-utopian tracts.

6. Gippius's attempts to trace the signs of Gogol's literary turning-point to "psychologism" at the beginning of the 40s are interesting.

7. The idea that Gogol burned part of *Dead Souls* by accident, and that for this reason it was not necessary to entertain the idea of the existence of any other final edition of the first volume, aside from "rough drafts" preserved by

chance, is hardly acceptable; but in any case it is best to make sure of this through a stylistic analysis of the remaining parts, something which has not yet been done.

There are, of course, in Gippius's book other minor but apt remarks, for example, on the precursors of *Evenings on a Farm*, on the types of tales in this anthology, on the elements of farce in Gogol's early novellas, and a few others. But they are less well developed and not always clearly formulated.

In general, Gippius's book, despite its methodological contradictions, is one of the best surveys of Gogol's creative work, not only in its successful summary of earlier achievements, but in adapting them to an independently conceived schema.

Chapter 3

In the last decade few scholars have addressed the history of plots in Gogol's poetics. A summary of the results achieved prior to 1914 was made by N. I. Korobka and V. V. Kallash in introductory articles and notes to the collection of Gogol's works which they edited. Gippius selected certain factual material for his discussion of the plot of *The Inspector General* and, in part, of *The Marriage* and "Notes of a Madman" in his book on Gogol.

Aside from Stender-Petersen's work, studies devoted to Gogol's plot structure are rare. It is hard to locate any system in them which would link them all in one pragmatic series. On the contrary, it is immediately apparent that these are chance manifestations of disparate interests.

Gogol's relationship to the tradition of composition and plot of both previous Russian literature and that of his own time has been almost completely ignored in recent years. Only the matter of the friendship between Gogol and Pushkin, with no study of their literary connections, has attracted interest.[13]

Among Gogol's other contemporaries, P. Svinin has attracted the attention of scholars as a "patron"; it was his person which provided Gogol with the character and plot material for the image of Khlestakov.[14] Gippius also mentioned, as sources for *Evenings on a Farm*, certain plots from the works of O. Somov, Olin ("Godfather's Bed"), Pogorelsky ("The Lafertova Poppyseed-cake Seller," 1825), and Polevoi ("Christmas Tales"). In general, it must be noted that the link between the Gogolian plot structure and the preceding Great Russian tradition, as well as the literary currents of Gogol's own time, remains unexamined. Only in Gippius did Gogol's comedies find a careful student of their plot structure; he viewed them against the background of early comedic and vaudevillian literature.

Another problem of plot structure which long has occupied scholars is Gogol's relationship to the Ukrainian literary tradition. Here the influence of Narezhny's novels and tales on Gogol always has been maintained.

In his article "V. T. Narezhny" (Chapter 2, "Narezhny and Gogol"),[15] Iu. M. Sokolov returned to the question and, leaving aside comparisons of "The Prince Beyond the Seas" to *The Inspector General*, and likewise "The Zaporozhets" to *Taras Bulba*, compared certain pictures of seminary life introduced by Narezhny and Gogol ("Bursak" with "Viy" and *Taras Bulba*, and "The Two Ivans" with "Viy").[16] The conclusion he reached: "Gogol made direct use of the novels of his predecessor, particularly as a source of ethnographic material. But... Gogol also used other sources, both written and, perhaps, oral tales and personal observations." The comparisons were made in the traditional fashion of textual comparisons.

There was still argument about Kvitka's influence on Gogol. N. Bazhenov compared certain features of the plot axis to which the image of Pliushkin was attached, with a description of the Miser in Kvitka's novel *The Adventures of Stolbikov* (V. Bazhenov, "G. F. Kvitka as an Inspirer of Gogol. On the Question of Literary Borrowing," 1916, Kharkov). There is no definite proof of an artistic link between *Dead Souls* and this novel; only a bare comparison of the texts, in the tradition of articles on "borrowings," is presented. Aizenshtok, in the article "On the Question of Literary Influence (Kvitka and Gogol)" re-examines the question of Kvitka's influence on Gogol and comes to a negative conclusion.[17]

One cannot say that the problem of influence was raised in a strikingly deep or original way in this article. Nevertheless, the majority of works on Gogol's plot structure revolve around this problem of literary influences, of Gogol's adaptation of plots and motifs from both contemporary and preceding Ukrainian, Russian and West European literature. At the same time, this is the sole theoretical article on Gogolian plot structure.

There have been no valuable studies of other aspects of the artistic relationships between Gogol and "writers of the Ukraine"; scholars have not succeeded in tracing the history of Gogol's plots against the background of both Russian literatures—Great and Little Russian. And thus, interest has grown in the findings on Gogol's links to West European literatures, primarily German.

Incidentally, S. Rodzevich, in the article "On the History of Russian Romanticism (E. T. A. Hoffmann and the 1830s and 1840s in our literature),"[18] touches on the problem of the reflection of Hoffmann's motifs in Gogol's work. In his opinion, Gogol's general aesthetic views in the article "Sculpture, Painting and Music" doubtlessly are imbued with the influence of Hoffmann. His comparisons, however, are extremely general. Yet Rodzevich points concretely to a series of motifs from Gogol's works, motifs which are easily found in Hoffmann. For instance, the "motif of the artist who has destroyed his talent," the motif of Gogol's "The Portrait," is encountered in Hoffmann's *The Elixirs of Satan,* in the chapter "From the Notes of an Ancient Artist." The common psychological figure of Francesco reminds Rodzevich of Chertkov. Rodzevich is prepared to compare the image of the money-lender with several characters from Hoffmann—with Albano from "The Magnetizer," with Koppelius from "The Sandman," and with Doctor Dapertutto from "The Lost Reflection." Thus, Gogol's "The Portrait" seems to Rodzevich to be knocked together from various planks taken from Hoffmann.

It is necessary to introduce the author's general conclusion, since it differs sharply from the results of similar studies by Stender-Petersen, who links a whole epoch of Gogol's work (ending with "The Nose") to the name of Hoffmann: "With the exception of 'The Portrait,' where Gogol's acquaintance with Hoffmann is more or less directly apparent, the points of overlap in the work of the author of *Dead Souls* and that of *The Serapion Brothers* has an incidental character; and if these points are interesting as brushstrokes in the picture of enthusiasm for Hoffmann in the 30s, in and of themselves they afford too little material to conclude that Hoffmann significantly influenced our writer."

Among foreign scholars, Stender-Petersen has devoted much attention to the study of plot in Gogol's work with respect to its ties with German literature. Three of his works have reached us: (1) "Johann Heinrich Voss und der junge Gogol. Ein Beitrag zur Seelenkunde Gogols" (*Zaertyl au Edda.* Bd. XV. Kristiana. 1921); (2) "Der Usprung des Gogolschen Teufels" (Ur Minnestofi norgiven av Filologiska samtun det i Göteborg. 1920; *Göteborgs Höskolas Arsstrift.* Bd. 26); (3) "Gogol und die deutsche Romantik" (*Euphorion. Zeitschrift für Literaturgeschichte.* XXIV. Drittes Heft 1922).

In the first article ("Joh. Hein. Voss und der junge Gogol") Stender-Petersen raises an issue which relates less to plot structure than to psychology: "to trace in Gogol's immature, aesthetically speaking, weak work" the stages of his psychological development, since "Gans Kiukhelgarten," in the opinion of the author, is as important a psychological document for an understanding of Gogol's first experiments as *The Inspector General* or *Dead Souls* are for an understanding of the essence of Gogol's poetic work and his spiritual development. To solve this problem, however, Stender-Petersen analyzes the idyll from the point of view of plot structure and composition, seeking to trace the process of its creation. He sees in it a series of stylistic layers acquired at different periods of time. The initial core of the idyll comprised the first, sixth, seventh and the conclusion of the last, eighteenth scene created under the influence of Voss's "Luise." They were begun at the end of the summer of 1827 in Vasilevska.

It is no accident that Gogol turned to Voss for inspiration. Gogol's youthful idyllic worldview, which was a reflection of the national element in his soul, is transparent here. Later, in the final reworking of the idyll in the summer of 1828 (upon graduation from the Nezhinsky Lycée), Gogol underwent the strong influence of Schiller and Tieck. "Only now does there appear the Romantic image of Gans Kiukhelgarten, with his melancholy and faithful reflection of the author's soul, and we see how the 'blue flower' of German Romanticism becomes comprehensible to the idyll's hero, so recently joyful and satisfied with everything."

But the concluding, reconciling motif is not from Tieck and Schiller; it could have come to Gogol from Zhukovsky's "Teona and Eskhina." Thus, "Gogol's psychological path of development ran from Voss to Tieck through Schiller."

In this Stender-Petersen article, neither the comparisons with Voss, nor the demonstrations of the influence of Schiller, Tieck and Zhukovsky are new. They had been made earlier by Sharovolsky, Kulman and others. What is new in the article is the treatment of Gogol's first idyll as a mechanical interweaving of two stylistically-distinct layers, and the raising of this duality of plot to two chronologically distinct moments. There is no need to link this facet of literary history with Gogol's spiritual side. But the idea of a mechanical fusing of separate, often alien pieces as a method of compositional blending in Gogol's work should be hailed (cf. "The Portrait").

Stender-Petersen's second work about the origin of Gogol's devil is linked by its negative conclusions alone to the problem of the "German" influence on Gogol. In it, Stender-Petersen elucidates the genesis of Gogol's conception of the devil and the plots connected with him. Their roots are found in Ukrainian folk beliefs. The author traces the "German" attire of Gogol's devil to Polish models in the Ukrainian folk rendering. Thus the motifs of "The Night before Christmas" are compared with the Faust legend about Twardowski. The literary-historical material here is scant, however, and the basic idea about the Polish influence is dubious.[19]

On the other hand, the article "Gogol und die deutsche Romantik" presents a wealth of material and new proposals. The author characterizes this period in Gogol's work as marked by a predisposition for German Romanticism, and, in the main, for two of its representatives: Tieck and Hoffmann.

The influence of Tieck is already reflected in the general tone of "Gans Kiukhelgarten." Beginning with *Evenings on a Farm* it had intensified and combined with the influence of Hoffmann, whose poetics Gogol tried mightily to overcome; he succeeds in parodically baring Hoffmann's basic principles in "The Overcoat" and in "The Nose." The element of the fantastic in Gogol's poetic contemplation of the world, an element which subsequently disappears without a trace, must be attributed wholly to the influence of German Romanticism.

Stender-Petersen also assembles parallels with Gogol's plots from the works of Tieck and Hoffmann. A portion of them, for example, "Tieck's *Liebeszauber*" (treated as the source of the plot of "Festival on the Eve of Ivan Kupala") and "Pietro von Avano" (related to "A Terrible Vengeance") already has been alluded to by earlier scholars. The sole new feature is the comparison of a series of motifs linked to the theme of a clan's curse in "A Terrible Vengeance" and Tieck's drama *Karl von Berneck.*

More numerous are the new parallels Stender-Petersen identifies in the plot structures of Gogol and Hoffmann. The comparisons of the structure of "A Terrible Vengeance" and Hoffmann's novella *Ignaz Denner* (originally *Revier-Jäger*) are very convincing. The image of the criminal sorcerer Denner, who kills his daughter Georgina's son after suddenly appearing in the house of his son-in-law; the depiction of the father-daughter relationship (in addition to the motif of their illicit love); Denner's attempts to coerce Georgina's husband to become involved with thieves—all this is reminiscent of similar situations in "A Terrible Vengeance." In Stender-Petersen's opinion, Gogol merely reworks Denner's plot, on the one hand, by complicating Tieck's motifs with Ukrainian local color, and, on the other, by making the motif of a father's illicit passion for his daughter (a motif, with which Hoffmann was not familiar), the pivot of the plot.

But it is precisely the dominant role of the motif of a father's illicit passion for his daughter which, because it springs directly from the "Frenetic literature" of French Romanticism, contradicts, to a significant degree, Stender-Petersen's construct of a Gogol who at the onset of the 30s was completely absorbed in the poetics of German Romanticism; in fact, Stender-Petersen continually examines Gogol's Petersburg tales from this angle alone. The comparisons of "Notes of a Madman" with the episode about Geheimsekretar Nettleman from the

"Fragmente aus dem Leben dreier Freunde," who fancied himself as König auf Amboina and conducted himself accordingly, are original. There is an unquestionable similarity between various scenes from Nettleman's story and the events described in Poprishchin's diary. But the incidental episode in Hoffmann, conveyed in the outsider's story, is taken by Gogol and placed in the frame of a clerk's life and clothed in the form of a madman's personal notes, i.e., it becomes an independent theme.

Stender-Petersen also attributes the fantastic ending of the novella "The Overcoat" to Hoffmann, but sees already a transformation of the purely aesthetic function of Hoffmannesque fantastic into an ethically symbolic one. In "Nevsky Prospect" the image of the artist Piskarev and individual details of his surrounding environment seem to Stender-Petersen to be close to the image of the dreamer Anselm from Hoffmann's novella *Der goldene Topf*. "The Nose" is cursorily compared with Hoffmann's novella *Mann ohne Spiegelbild* (which already had been done earlier by Russian Gogol scholars).

Gogol's tale "The Portrait" is examined in the light of Hoffmann's poetics in a more attentive and detailed fashion. Stender-Petersen traces the central motif to "Fragmente aus dem Leben dreier Freunde." Here, in the stories of Alexander and Martsell, the images of phantoms emerge and the appearance before Alexander of a long, thin figure with a deathly pale face and flashing evil eyes is, in the opinion of Stender-Petersen, reminiscent of a corresponding scene with Chertkov.

"The Portrait," however, appears to Stender-Petersen to be tied to Hoffmann's work by far stronger threads than the chance coincidence of motifs. "The Portrait," he writes, "was the expression of the tortured doubts of an artist who was seeking a new form suited to his talent. The gripping horror which the portrait of Petromikhali evoked in the artist Chertkov was also felt by Gogol when he glanced at Hoffmann's art . . ." Stender-Petersen even places into Gogol's mouth a tirade about "frightful reality," seeing in "The Portrait" an overcoming of Hoffmann and a renunciation of the fantastic in the Romantic style. There was no congeniality between

Hoffmann and Gogol. They had completely different poetic natures and diametrically opposed artistic paths. The refined, extravagant Hoffmann was an enthusiast and mystificator, whereas the idealistic dreamer Gogol, through conscious imitation of the poetics of Tieck and Hoffmann, moved toward a bitter acknowledgement of real life, and a cold reproduction of it.

The period of imitating Hoffmann, embracing the years from 1832 through 1834, is the period of Gogol's lack of freedom and independence. It is a time of the formulation of his own personal style while still enchained and struggling to overcome the poetics of German Romanticism, and especially Hoffmann.

In Stender-Peterson's article there are many valuable indications of Gogol's dependence upon Hoffmann. But it is impossible to accept the author's schema, in which a large segment of Gogol's work preceding the final formation of his "natural" style is placed in direct and exclusive proximity to German Romanticism.

In this schema no recognition is given to the influences upon Gogol which came from other quarters—not only from Russian literature and folklore, but from foreign, and particularly French, literature. In general, the problem of the tie between Gogol's work and that French literature which so excited the aesthetic tastes of Russian writers and critics of the 30s has not been raised in research on Gogol. Even Gogol's French admirers have not engaged the problem; in Louis Leger's book on Gogol not a single mention of it is made.

There is no need to expatiate on Louis Leger's book: *Nicolas Gogol* (1914). For the Russian reader, the only new things, perhaps, are (1) the suggestion of an unreal synthesis of landscape details in Gogol's depictions of nature in "Old World Landowners": "le melon ne mûrit pas au moment ou le merisier est en heur et l'on ne commence pas à conserver des poires et des pommes au temps des cerises"; (2) the denial of any possible plot similarities between *Taras Bulba* and Merimée's tale "Mateo Falcone"; (3) fleeting mention of the possible use of a play by Kotzebue, *La petite ville*, in Gogol's work on the first act of *The Inspector General*.

Aside from this, there is a curious chapter, "Gogol and Merimée," in which Louis Leger speaks about Merimée's interest in Gogol, and about his lack of understanding of the text of Gogol's works; he suggests models for his "translation" of *The Inspector General* into French.[20]

Notwithstanding the paucity of work on Gogolian plot structure, it is still necessary to acknowledge that it is this field which has attracted scholars most of all, and that it is here that the results of study are most evident. In the study of plot structures the comparative-historical method has fully predominated. The general problems of plot construction in Gogol's work—alien motifs and plots serving as devices of composition, the replacement of various plot tendencies in Gogol's poetics, in a word, questions of a more complex order which go beyond the sphere of bare comparisons—have not interested scholars. For this reason it has been necessary to speak solely about new material, rather than about new ideas, in this chapter on the studies of plot structure.

Only one conclusion can be drawn from a survey of all the more or less valuable works on Gogol, namely the conclusion presented at the beginning of this survey: Gogol's poetics have not been studied and established. In view of this, I have decided to present a brief summary of my own observations on the forms of Gogol's work. In summarizing my own observations I shall be attempting not so much to reproduce fully the results of my work on particular aspects of Gogol's poetics and stylistics, but to construct a certain general schema of Gogol's work.

Chapter 4

It is no accident that Gogol's first published work was in poetic form, and an outmoded, archaic form at that for the time when his "Gans Kiukhelgarten" appeared. Poetry, more than anything else, corresponded to his notion of a "lyrical and serious genre," and to his predilection for sound effects and rhetoric. According to Annenkov, Derzhavin always remained Gogol's literary idol. Furthermore, the poetics of Sentimentalism became an organic part of Gogol's artistic world and, as one of its basic components, was always ready to blossom forth, despite the fact that as early as "The Bloody Bandura Player" Gogol earnestly sought to check this impulse. Along with this there appeared, from his very first steps, vague and incompletely assimilated echoes of Romanticism in its contradictory forms, as well as the imitation of Pushkin and Zhukovsky. In Gogol's creative consciousness, Classicism, Sentimentalism, and Romanticism coexisted as parallel, but unequal, stylistic forms. Even Gogol's first poem betrayed his artistic eclecticism: it was fused together from alien, heterogeneous pieces woven, transparent seams and all, into one multi-colored blanket. In an epoch of general passion for poetry, Gogol dedicated himself to reworking verse forms. This was characteristic for him. Gogol always trod an artistic path whose basic lines already had been marked, outstripping everyone on it, and lending even sharper embodiment to already mature tendencies.

Gogol's first experiment, however, is curious not only because, despite all of its provincialism, it already portrayed Gogol as a cunning rag-and-bones merchant, a tailor of various literary forms and genres, but due to another, purely literary reason. In this work the two linguistic elements that characterized Gogol's style were clearly revealed in all their incohesiveness and limitations: common, vulgar, conversational speech, and solemn, bookish, Church-Slavic language. These two forms of language remained unreconciled in the poem, destroying its semantic wholeness and emotional harmony:

> Why did secret despair
> *Pass* throughout my soul?
>
> Old chestnut trees stand all around,
> Bending their branches, as *if they want*
> *To fight their way into the windows*. .
> Is this the way one passes to eternal rest?
>
> A corpse in a white shroud
> Slowly rises,
> The good fellow pompously
> Chafes his dusty bones. . .
>
> In reveries she
> Stared at the autumn night. . .
> *The object is one and the same*. . .
>
> And our old men *chatter*. .
> And the youth boil in dances. . .

The two streams of Gogolian language are revealed here, albeit faintly: (1) that lofty bookish, archaic speech which departed from contemporary artistic forms and approached the traditions of the turn of the eighteenth and nineteenth centuries, straining the metaphorical rhetoric of early Romanticism; and (2) that coarse, vulgar, everyday speech which still had not been integrated into literary locution and even stood in opposition to its established norms—a semi-intellectual speech with a touch of Ukrainian.

But reform of the literary language is what Gogol thinks about least of all in his idyll. He is concerned here with the blending of genres and manners of depiction. His stylistic elements proved to be ill-adapted to poetic form; this decided the fate of Gogol's first literary experiment. Moreover, in general Gogol's position in relation to the high Sentimental-Romantic style was predetermined. Gogol still does not command it freely; it is beyond his powers of artistic transformation. Even in his prose experiments, when practicing the high style, Gogol selects those themes around which a rich symbolism had already firmly formed. It would have been more appropriate for him to subject his language to new combinations, to complicate the syntactical forms of its metaphorical intersections (cf. his article: "Woman") in an archaic manner. Thus Gogol was fated to stand outside the forms of the literary language of his time: he was able to be either an archaist, or a democrat-innovator. And the problem of the linguistic organization of various literary genres quickly pushed compositional and plot-related thematical tasks into the background for Gogol. His inclination in this direction is most prominent in *Evenings on a Farm near Dikanka*; this also represented an attempt to blend genres. The general direction of Gogol's work, however, was, in this sense, predetermined by the preceding tradition of the Russian imitators of Walter Scott. They are characterized by their contemporary (Bulgarin) in this manner: "Walter Scott gained renown under fictitious names which, finally, merged in the sobriquet of the great stranger (le grand inconnu). For us it also began with this. The author conceals his name beneath fictitious sobriquets and requests his friends to announce the great secret at each postal station, but the journalists he allows to guess, and pronounces his real name in riddles. After this *prank* the matter begins. There should be nationality (*narodnost'*) in the novel. Yet, what is 'nationality'? Let's take a look at Walter Scott. The action occurs in Scotland, hence, the action will be set in Russia. In Walter Scott's work the peasants, lackeys and soldiers converse a great deal among themselves using provincialisms and common speech—and the matter doesn't stop there for us. One has only to think up a beginning: for this there is history and forgotten fairy-tales, and then a homegrown Walter Scott, like Balzac, sets to work." (*The Northern Bee*, 1831, No. 286).

Further, Bulgarin traces the endless "chatter of interpolated characters and common speech in conversations," and the "faithful copying of gutter eloquence" to this same literary tradition. Of course, there were counter-tendencies which sprang up organically in the process of the struggle between various artistic systems and made it possible for this influence to be felt and a corresponding literary tradition to arise on Russian soil.

Among those vying systems, the main ones were those which were nourished by popular plots and popular poetic devices, and those which strove toward the frozen form of literary bookish language as a counterpose to dialectical, conversational, everyday "common speech."[21]

The narrative devices of Walter Scott were developed on Russian soil by Somov (cf. his "Kikimora,"—a story of a *peasant* on the high road,[22] and others); Pogodin (cf. his short story: "Petrus"[23] with popular Ukrainian forms of speech, as well as his tale "Epilepsy" and others);[24] Polevoi ("Christmas Tales") and a series of other lesser writers of the 20s and 30s.

In his critique of M. Pogodin's tale, "Epilepsy," Polevoi was prepared to trace a history of the new *Russian* tale and novel from the successors of Walter Scott: "The new excitement dates from our acquaintance with Walter Scott. His success, the entertaining quality of his works, and the novelty of his art attracted the attention of Russian writers. They sought the sources of this entertaining quality in Walter Scott's novels, and expected to find it in the national element and in the miniature depiction of details prevalent in his novels. Turning their attention to the Russian way of life, our novelists saw that we, too, had our own locales, our own events, our own tales and sayings: they were brought out on the stage and thus a conception about Russian tales and perhaps even about Russian novels was formed."[25] On top of all this, one must add that Walter Scott's theoretical articles enjoyed great popularity: "On the Miraculous in the Novel" (in *The Son of the Fatherland*, 1829) and "On Demonology and Witches" (in the *Moscow Telegraph*, 1830, 35-36).

The influence of Walter Scott and his Russian admirers was expressed in Gogol's work not only in his use of ethnic Ukrainian material, fairy tales and legends, but also in the general manner of the "provincial" skaz, which is particularly obvious in the composition of *Evenings*. The image of Rudyi Panko as the publisher of *Evenings*, his "forewords" acquainting the reader with his "narrators," his remarks on various novellas, even the composition of the tales themselves replete with epigraphs to the chapters—all this had its roots in the "novels" of Walter Scott.

The entire genre of forewords by an interpolated publisher who assembles the "stories" of his neighbors and friends became widespread in Russian literature under the influence of Walter Scott's "forewords," in which Jedadiah Cleishbotham played the especially vivid roll of the "school-master and parish clerk of Gandercleuch." The character Pasichnik is doubtlessly akin to him. One need only compare the "foreword" to *Evenings* with the foreword to "The Scottish Puritans" and "Edinburgh Dungeons" to be reassured of this. Other Scott forewords, for example, the forewords to *The Monastery, The Fortunes of Nigel,* and so forth, provided Gogol with material for his mosaic scenes. Thus, Gogol clearly sided with the tradition of Russian admirers of Walter Scott not only in his choice of artistic material, in his devices, in the manner of skaz (provincial and out of the way, with a tendency toward dramatized action), but even in the manner of compositionally joining novellas by means of the image of a publisher hospitably assembling a circle of story-tellers.

It is curious that Gogol took the term "evenings," which was attached to Dikanka, Pasichnik's home, on compositional grounds, from the tradition of the almanacs established under French influence in the eighteenth century (for example, *Melancholy Evenings or a Collection of Merry and Instructive Tales by Sundry French Writers*, Moscow. 1787; *Evenings Before a Fireplace or a Collection of Fairytales and Comedies for Children.* In French and Russian on opposite pages. Moscow. 1811). It is clear that it is not so much plots and their compositional formation that now engaged Gogol, so much as the manner of the telling of the tale, the construction of dialogue and stylistic forms.

In *Evenings on a Farm near Dikanka* the interlacing of two poetic styles which had undergone individual artistic deformation was clearly revealed. The first, the patriarchal-familial, skaz, vulgar-conversational style of a neighbor's conversation, which reflected the influence of Walter Scott and his Russian epigones, was in essence a form of comedic monologue. To judge by the comic lexical and syntactical devices, it did not at all differ from the formulas of common speech. Gogol skillfully introduced in it provincial Ukrainian, dialectical, and semi-intellectual speech combinations, akin to the traditions of the interludes, Ukrainian comedies and novellas (Kvitka), and linked it to the comical figures of the village sages, Rudyi Panko, the clerk Foma Grigorevich, and Stepan Ivanovich Kurochka. The popular fairy-tale anecdotal plots and everyday chatter fit easily into this style (cf. on the one hand the "foreword" to *Evenings* and, on the other, "The Enchanted Spot" and "The Missing Letter").

But it was only through this medium that the plot with tragic tones and Romantic strivings took shape, as in "The Festival on the Eve of Ivan Kupala"; his style began to fluctuate, becoming complicated with elements that were not at all amenable to its basic core.

In connection with this style, which in no way differs from the style of fragments of "A May Night" and even of certain passages in "A Terrible Vengeance," there is a popular poetic stream in the novella in the conversation of the pair of lovers.

Thus, the style of familiar neighborly chatter with a comic underscoring of the substandard speech forms common in everyday practice revealed its suitability as a form of anecdotal skaz or comedic dialogue as early as *Evenings on a Farm*. This was a natural starting point in the direction of the comedy-farce about which Gogol had been thinking since 1832. On the other hand, this style presented itself as potential material for play with the skaz manner, for the illusory change of speaking masks behind which the author concealed himself, for the stylistic "affectation of a farcical jester." Gogol begins experiments with him, depsychologizing him, that is, freeing him from a supporting role as a vehicle for the description of psychological images—Rudyi Panko, Foma Grigorevich, and so forth. In "The Tale about How Ivan Ivanovich Quarrelled with Ivan Nikiforovich" the provincial style stands out as one of the author's stylistic masquerades, being replaced by other forms of skaz narration which cannot be reconciled in the single psychological image of Rudyi Panko. Futhermore, it was precisely on the basis of this linguistic stream that Gogol strove to work out those devices of "natural" and "portrait" depiction which contrasted with the manner of Sentimental-Romantic idealization then dominant. Consequently, a revolution occurred here, not only in the literary language, and not only in the opposition of the dialectical and basically vulgar-conversational common speech with its "coarse" words, variegated, non-normative syntax and its pathological formations to the lexical and syntactical clichés of the "Classical" literary, bookish language; there also was the formation of a new system of the stylistic reproduction of "nature," a system which depended upon the preceding "dirty" genres (the work of Izmailov, Narezhny, and others), on the Shandyism of Sterne, on the vaudeville-farcical tradition, on the Ukrainian puppet theater, on the newspaper miscellany and the "vulgar" anecdote.

Gogol, however, did not proceed by a direct route. Parallel to his work on vulgar skaz conversational elements, and comic transformations of the formulas of the "high" style, Gogol resorted to diverse variations of the Romantic style, transforming them and complicating their ancillary elements. In *Evenings on a Farm* he first places forms of the Romantic style into the mouth of a "buffoon," anticipating them through comic description in the person of the "publisher," Rudyi Panko: "It would happen that he would raise one finger, and looking at the end of it would go on to relate elegantly and cunningly, as in printed books. Another time one listens, listens, and a reflective mood sets in. One can't for the life of him understand. Where did he get hold of such words?" And later, "on this account" Foma Grigorevich's splendid introduction is presented. However, looking more closely at these "tales" attributed to the "ingenious" narrator, it is easily noted that the "Romantic element" in them is but a frame; the central part is either farcical comedy as in "The Fair at Sorochinsk," or tragi-comic as in "A May Night," where a young pair is enveloped in the layers of fantastic-song styles and the plot. The "Romantic" (in the proper sense) style in both tales merely forms the emotionally charged, "phonetic" landscapes, in which the style of Sentimental pathos is abruptly broken off, to be replaced suddenly either by the everyday-comic, "coarse," provincial language of conversation ("The Fair at Sorochinsk," "A May Night," chapter 2) or song-like measured, lyrical dialogue.

The type of novella which predominated in the 20s and 30s reflected the influence of Byron and Sterne in its fragmentary composition; in Gogol this type of composition acquires an uncommon form of alternately comic and tragic dramatic segments with a "landscape overture," brief remarks from the director, and "static" portraits. A sharpness in the change of voices is the characteristic trait of these "tales." In the conclusion, the lyrical ending casts new emotional light on the entire "drama."

However, in general these devices of construction did not meet with sympathy. The attempt to elevate the Sentimental pathetic element of the Romantic style and to dissolve contradictory metaphorical linkages ("The aimlessly strolling oaks stand. . .beneath the clouds. . ," "the woods stopped in immobile inspiration. . ,"etc.) in complex melodic modulations met with particular disfavor. Polevoi greeted the attempt to veil the mosaic-like, 'material,' multi-partite scene of emotionally-charged musical language as an "incomprehensibly lofty flight." And Gogol renounced it temporarily, returning to the lyrical introduction, to "soundlessly crackling tirades," but replacing the emotionally-charged landscape with "personal," Sentimental confessions only in *Dead Souls* (Senkovsky). Now he removes the "buffoon" from the stage:. . ."The Buffoon, who spoke such an affected language that even many Moscow wits could not understand it, has not been around for a long time. . . ."

In general, the new narrators of the second part of *Evenings* are oriented toward the provincial skaz tradition with its familiar, neighborly tone; they have only slightly adapted it to the forms of the "Classical," literary bookish language, instilling in it (especially in descriptions of beautiful women and nature) a primitive and Romantic symbolism. "A Terrible Vengeance" is an exception in this regard. Here Gogol presented his reform of the romantic style by grafting onto it the symbolism and rhythms of folk poetry and the Ukrainian heroic epics. These elements, which until that time had adorned only the language of lovers, now became a part of all the stylistic forms of the tale.

In "A Terrible Vengeance," however, it was not only a new functional correspondence of poetic styles—revealed earlier in Gogol's poetics—that became evident; the author's leaning in the direction of the Romantically-horrific style could be vaguely perceived in it. Up until this time, Gogol's poetics had been nourished on juices which ran from *Sentimental genres seasoned with German Romanticism*: Ukrainian folk poetry, the Nativity scenes of the Ukrainian puppet theater, as well as the works of Walter Scott and his Russian admirers. But in "A Terrible Vengeance" those motifs resound which doubtlessly date from the poetics of the "Frenetic school" (the motif of the illicit passion of a father for his daughter, and daughter-killing). The accumulation of horror scenes in the spirit of French Romanticism was reflected in the style of the tale, uniting with its unique devices expressions of emotion ("his voice, like a knife, nicked the heart". . ."fear and cold cut into his Cossack veins". . ."he cried out as if someone had begun to saw his yellow bones". . ."it would still be a kindness if they would boil him alive in a cauldron or flay his sinful hide," and so forth), and evoking a stream of "frightful," gloomy epithets ("wild, "frenzied," "furious," "inhuman," and others).

The "Frenetic school" and its offshoots immediately must have seized Gogol's attention, since the Romantic-horrific style appeared to him to be the antithesis of Sentimentalism. The farcical Nativity tradition, exercises in the provincial style in the manner of provincial "literati" à la Walter Scott, the mechanization of the animate adopted from the "puppet" theater and maintained by the influence of Hoffmann—all this with its comically simplified, physiological "corporeality" contradicted the psychological tasks of Sentimentalism. And Gogol, having assimilated these traditions in *Evenings on a Farm*, with his own peculiar tendency toward maximum sharpness, had to lay bare their essence and find himself an antagonist of Sentimentalism. Yet, this was a low genre (cf. "The Tale of Two

Ivans").

The school of Romantic-horror, which first interested Gogol solely due to the engaging quality of the plots in its frightening stories, now responded to new stylistic tendencies taking form in his poetics in the realm of "lower" genres. Now, the romantic-horror style seemingly posed parallel courses for him in the realm of "high" art. From 1832 on clear traces of a profound interest in "Frenetic" poetics may be seen in Gogol's works. Now he borrows basic material for his plots in Jules Janin's novel-manifesto: *The Dead Ass and the Headless Woman,*[26] in the works of Victor Hugo ("boundless in his greatness"), Sue, Maturin, and other writers regarded by literati of the 30s as belonging to the "Frenetic" school. Following their precepts and principles one moment, then engaging in a fervent polemic against them the next, Gogol worked out all of his devices of depiction which later became part of the poetics of the "Natural School."

Gogol was not alone in his fascination with "Frenetic" literature; on the contrary, the period between 1832-35 was a time of its rousing success. Walter Scott ceded literary pre-eminence to Victor Hugo—in the minds of Russian literati. The conservative camp, i.e., the journals *The Northern Bee, The Library for Reading,* and *Son of the Fatherland*, became alarmed and defended ennobled "nature" and the devices of Sentimental-Romantic idealization. Yet while Gogol shared the general interests of the innovators, all the same he was a solitary and original figure in the way he transformed the principles of "Frenetic" poetics.

It is necessary to trace briefly Gogol's course in this direction. "The Bloody Bandura Player" is the immature experiment of an apprentice. In this work not only the motifs and situations (a gloomy night, a dungeon where a man with flayed skin is concealed, a scene of torture), but the style (the rhythmically-charged epithets, the symbolism of death enveloping everything, both natural and man-made, language interrupted by horrified exclamations), the then-popular formulas of "Frenetic" feelings, in a word, all the accessories of "Frenetic" poetics were incorporated directly, with no attempt at synthesizing them with outside influences, or subjecting them to any significant, individual revision. Yet this literary cult of physical torture and torment, a cult of artificially convulsive and rhetorically pompous style, did not attract Gogol for long. Another aspect of "Frenetic poetics" began to interest him: the combination of strange and humorous elements, the clownish and comic with the monstrous and horrible, the grotesque scene. From the Ukrainian folk tradition influenced by the provincial interlocutors of Walter Scott, Gogol arrived at the detailed reproduction of everyday, "banal" life, which had received a new stylistic basis and new compositional forms in the legacy of the Frenetic school, for example, in Jules Janin's novel. Now Gogol devoted himself to a synthetic revision of the Romantic-horror style. Sometimes he combined this style with forms from the earlier "Walter Scott" manner, and with old Romantic forms in the fashionable genre of the historical novel (*Taras Bulba*); at other times he applied the devices of "Frenetic" depiction to the folk and Romantic fantastic in conjunction with stylistic forms which he had elaborated earlier ("Viy"). At still other times he instilled antithetic artistic tendencies in old Sentimental genres ("Old World Landowners"). Here it is necessary to dwell for a moment on the characteristics of certain stages in Gogol's involvement with Frenetic poetics.

In *Taras Bulba* the "Frenetic" plot composition is clear. The three plot lines are the fates of Taras Bulba, Ostap, and Andrii. Each of them has a tragic demise: one commits suicide, one is executed, and one is burned at the stake. A gloomy nocturnal landscape serves as the background for frightful events throughout the novel. In certain scenes, for example, in the scene of the drowning of the Jews, and in the picture of Ostap's execution, an adherence to Victor Hugo's principle of combining "buffoonery" and "horror" is immediately apparent. As in the novels of Hugo and Sue, the description of the hero's execution always contains echoes of comic crowd scenes. In one touching yet horrifying execution scene, Gogol interjects comic characters: a Polish gentleman and his paramour Iuzysia. There are other parallels as well; Gogol, however, does not submit entirely to "Frenetic" poetics. He renounces some of its tendencies: the detailed, "anatomical" reproduction of torture, torment and murder; and he rejects its devices for depicting the emotions of horror, lessening and independently revising the common forms of the Romantic-horror style. "I will not disturb the reader with a picture of hellish torments which would make his hair stand on end," the author avows in *Taras Bulba*. This represented a victory of the Walter Scott tradition over the principles of "Romantic horror." In "Viy" existing folk-Romantic forms, which Gogol perceived under the banner of Walter Scott and which had been interwoven with Ukrainian folk-poetic and bookish German Romantic traditions, were synthesized with the poetics of the Frenetic school in another manner, with a bias toward the devices of horror depiction and with greater attention toward the uniting of various forms of style. The compositional core of *Taras Bulba* was taken from "horrific romanticism," but other "Walter Scott" devices of depiction and stylistic forms were strung onto it. In "Viy" the folk-fantastic canvas was chosen in the old spirit of German Romanticism and the Russian "Walter Scott" tradition, but it was complicated with the Frenetic manner of depiction and with Frenetic forms of style in the tragic half of the tale.

Contemporaries did not appreciate the innovative synthesis in "Viy." They saw in it only an adaptation of Gogol's earlier stylistic tendencies to the new "Frenetic" poetics. "In 'Viy' there is neither end nor beginning nor idea; there is nothing other than a few frightening and improbable scenes"—wrote *The Library for Reading*. Shevyrev charged Gogol with a propensity for the detailed reproduction of psychic horrors: "The horrible visions of a seminarist...do not produce horror, because they are described in excessive detail. The horrible cannot be presented in detail...." Otherwise, "the horrible turns into the monstrous" (*The Moscow Observer*, 1835, No. 1).

Thus, contemporaries noted that Gogol combined "Frenetic" forms in every possible way, seeking to link them with antithetical stylistic constructions. Gogol is searching for "a new nature" distinguishable from the one created by the devices of Sentimental Romantic idealization. In addition, he renounced the "horrible reality" of the "Frenetic" novelists. His doleful idyll, "The Old-World Landowners," has special significance as an illustration of this quest. Gogol did not mount his struggle to destroy Sentimental forms merely by counterposing these forms with new opposing genres. It was in another fashion that he overcame Sentimentalism, by revising its forms or incorporating them into other, contrasting milieux (cf. the end of "The Tale of Two Ivans"). An old, but still popular and vital Sentimental genre, the idyll, is chosen for "Old-World Landowners," with all its compositional and stylistic attributes. But new, contrasting motifs, both comic and ironic, and stylistic constructions are introduced into it ("...you, it's true, would find a *smile entirely too cloying* for her kind face..." "Then his face, *one might say*, breathed with kindness..." and so forth). The general devices for describing everyday life, the manner of depicting characters and actions, the style of "portraits" of an entire, vivid milieu of "old men," the fleeting signs of an ironic evaluation of the heroes' lives, all comprised seemingly a special stylistic layer imposed on Sentimental forms for purposes of contrast and their destruction. Alongside these two contrasting tendencies, which become ever more charged towards the end of the tale, there sounded a third tendency with its origins in "Frenetic" poetics.

With regard to the plot, this tendency was reflected in the tragic denouement. Stylistically, it comprised entire pathetic tirades ("I knew him as a lover tenderly, passionately, furiously, boldly, secretly...." and so forth; "But, I confess that if the most violent and stormy night, with all the hell of the elements, overcame me, alone, in the midst of an impenetrable forest, I would not be so frightened of it as I would of a frightful calm in the midst of a cloudless day..."). At the same time, Gogol reveals a new side in the poetic ideology of the "Frenetic" school in "Old-World Landowners"—"the tragedy of trivial incidents." In "The Bloody Bandura Player" he was fascinated by the horrors of bloody torments and tortures; in *Taras Bulba* he set forth his individual, artistic emendations for this manner of depiction; in "Viy" he carried out an experiment in the reproduction of psychic torments, spiritual sufferings and outright panic. In "Old-World Landowners" the tragedy of extraordinary scenes and circumstances is replaced with the horror of daily happenstance: "My narrative comes closer to the totally sad event which changes forever the life of this peaceful little corner. The event will seem even more striking in that it arose from the most trivial incident. But by a strange order of things, insignificant causes have always given birth to great events and, on the contrary, great undertakings have ended in insignificant consequences..." Thus, Gogol's interest more and more is drawn to the tragedy of the banal, everyday anecdote, which unexpectedly springs from the mire of petty existence. In this work "Frenetic" poetics overlaid and combined with Gogol's previously formed artistic principles.

Gogol's first step towards the synthesis of two artistic systems, the first of which took shape as early as "The Tale of Two Ivans," and the second of which had been slowly formulated during Gogol's act of overcoming the dominant devices in the "Frenetic" depiction of nature, was the tale "Nevsky Prospect."

In this work there are two contrasting compositional series with respect to plot: one has its origins in motifs dating back to the works of the leaders of Romantic horror (Jules Janin, Balzac, and others), but is vested in the stylistic forms of Sentimental-Romantic idealization; the other represents a reworking of the anecdote in vaudevillian-farcical tones which already could be heard distinctly in "The Tale of Two Ivans." Both of these series, placed in contrasting parallel, became a part of the newspaper feuilleton about contemporary Petersburg, all three series symbolically united in the motif of deception. This is undoubtedly the most "complete" of Gogol's works, since it synthesizes all the forms of styles which comprised his poetics. Aside from the effects of contrast and devices of grotesque hyperbole, nothing in "Nevsky Prospect" is reminiscent of the basic Russian variants of the Romantic-horror style. On the contrary, the favorite plots of the "Frenetic" novella received a wholly new interpretation here. Gogol leaves only the bare banality of everyday "nature" in his work, casting off all the other themes and spheres of depiction which earlier had drawn him to Jules Janin and Victor Hugo.

Gogol underscored his break with "Frenetic" poetics with the novella "The Portrait," where the actual problem of "horrible reality" is posed.[27] He then sets out on an independent path. That "nature" which he selects as the focus of his artistic work was far from "ideal"—and no less far from its Romantic-horror variant. Gogol found it in the vulgar, sometimes "dirty" (from the point of view of the outmoded high tradition) anecdote, in the newspaper-journal miscellany, in the vaudeville-farce repertoire, and in its predecessors from the low literary genres. The love intrigue is swept aside or parodied. Virtuous heroes are eliminated.

The tales "The Nose" and "The Carriage" represent attempts at working out these new artistic tendencies. Under the banner of "Shandyism" on the canvas of the Romantic-fantastic, Gogol marked out their "dirty" patterns, using sensational journalistic accounts and popular anecdotes surrounded by less than modest associations.[28] *The Moscow Observer* refused to print the tale "The Nose" on account of its "dirty" content. But this was only a trial run: the new patterns had been embroidered on the old Sternian canvas. Before Gogol there now stood the task of objectifying stylistic forms, that is, freeing them from narrative masks along the lines of Panko.

The method of creating a new "nature" was not completely reconciled with this tendency. Indeed, it consisted of a complex system of the devices of grotesque hyperbole and the comic, disordered piling-up of elements of "reality." This "distortion" of the real world was realized most easily by means of an interpolated prism. Yet it was precisely this prism that Gogol was now trying to conceal. Earlier it had stood out clearly, was labeled as such, and sometimes even had a psychological realization (the image of Rudyi Panko). In "The Tale of Two Ivans," and partly in "Nevsky Prospect" and "The Nose," Gogol had begun to depsychologize those comic devices which were linked originally to specific characters, and to transfer them to other realms of language from the dialect milieu. Now Gogol was convinced that it was most convenient to hide the distorting mirror during the dramatic reproduction of action.

Gogol was drawn to drama, not only by his native Ukrainian traditions, and not only by the legacy of Walter Scott and Victor Hugo, but also by an awareness of the need to reform the literary language by orienting it toward "common speech," toward provincial and professional jargons, and toward the stagnant, defective formations of conversational, everyday, vulgar language.

It is natural that now, having set forth on *his own* path, and having found *his own* view of nature and *his own* devices for its formation after a long period of searching, Gogol focused all of his artistic interest on the comic farce, on *The Inspector General*; it was both the acme and the beginning of Gogol's independent path, the artistic realization of the principles of "Naturalism." It is understandable that the work's failure to achieve recognition dealt a painful blow to Gogol, who, lacking the strength to reject his own poetic system, now sought a way out by turning again to the Sentimental-Romantic tradition and linking certain of its elements to "natural poetics." Gogol again undertook to elaborate the forms of a "high" style in "Rome." In the first half of *Dead Souls* he found an illusory reconciliation of these two antithetical artistic systems. Reproducing "nature" by the methods and principles of Naturalism, Gogol concealed the "narrator" as a set character, thereby hiding his own authorial persona, and showing the reader the grimaces of various masks only in puns and language play.

In *Dead Souls* there is no skaz and no psychological image of the narrator. Conversational elements appear only sporadically, momentarily accompanied by an inconstant visage which immediately disappears. This creates the illusion that a humorously selected "nature" has been objectively reproduced. An "assembly of monsters" results, which, however, is shown as existing objectively and not generated by the distorting consciousness of the narrator. The author thus assumes responsibility only for the choice of heroes and elements of daily life, and not for the means of their artistic embodiment. In keeping with the imitation of objective depiction, general devices of style are fixed around two central tasks. The first is the reproduction of the heroes' *own* unique speech, with all its defective, alogical and "dirty" expressions, such that an illusion of photographic accuracy is achieved. The "vividness" of the elements should push the principle of artificial selection into the background here. The second central goal of the artist is to deprive the narrative style, or rather, the various forms of the narrative style, of psychological motivation. These forms should be so psychologically and linguistically heterogeneous, that beyond them it would be impossible to sense a single image, a single narrating presence. For this reason, the narrative style of *Dead Souls* is composed of a mixture of the various forms of conversational and written language, which produce the impression of a complex linguistic mosaic. Thus, in *Dead Souls* Gogol frees himself from the mask of a narrator, taking refuge only in the purely linguistic alternation of various forms of speech behind which one senses no psychological image. And all the heroes, all "nature" in the narration is seen to be objectively presented, and not distorted by the consciousness of a narrator. An illusion of genuinely "crooked mugs" is created since the reflecting, "crooked mirror" is veiled, or concealed. Such is "Naturalism." Gogol, however, is not completely hidden. On the contrary, he dons the guise of "Sentimental" exalted nature and begins to interrupt the objective stylistic reproductions with lyrical outpourings. In this manner "the author," it would seem, numbers among the heroes of the narrative; he evaluates "nature" from the Sentimental-moral point of view, gives himself over to dreams, pines about youth, and, in a word, does everything ascribed to the canon of Sentimentalism. This second stylistic stream must burst headlong into the basic natural layer: there may be no transitions between them since the devices of Naturalistic depiction are bared in the first volume of *Dead Souls*, without any adaptation to the elements of Sentimentalism. This was a mechanical fusion of contrasting artistic forms. Gogol's descent to Sentimentalism had begun.

The problem of synthesizing Sentimentalism with the "Natural" manner became the tormenting artistic riddle over which Gogol racked his brains until his death. Passing through the crucible of a "Naturalism" which rose in reaction to

Sentimental forms, Gogol was not able once again to become a Sentimentalist, although he was drawn in this direction by hostile criticism, contemporary literary currents, and even by his own religious and moral convictions. But he began to surrender one after another his former literary positions to Sentimentalism. In "The Overcoat," the touching episode expressed in the forms of the Sentimental-pathetic style appears as one of the organic components of the plot, tightly linked to the other "Naturalistic" elements of the tale. These are no longer "Naturalistic" scenes, but the partially Sentimental structure of the plot and theme themselves. The general tone of the entire story changes decisively; laughter due to the proximity of the "pitiful" episode seems to sound through tears. The contrast between the Sentimental-pathetic notes and the dominant tone of "comic taunts," however, appears to be so sharp that the unifying of these two language forms into a single narrative image could only be forced and mechanical. This does not satisfy Gogol. Sentimental forms are now made the basis of his artistic constructions; natural elements are only infused in and adapted to them. He writes a Sentimental utopia, *Selected Passages from Correspondence with Friends*. In the second volume of *Dead Souls*, where the traces of his incessant, stubborn struggle between an instinctive propensity for Naturalism and his "attraction" for Sentimentalism are sketched out, Gogol's inability to combine Sentimental civic moralism with a Naturalistic manner of presenting "lower themes" undoubtedly was revealed. The destroyer of Sentimental traditions vainly sought to resurrect and reconcile them to those stylistic tendencies in whose name the Sentimental forms earlier had been repudiated. For Gogol this task was inherently unrealizable; it was realized later by Dostoevsky. Gogol vacillated in torment between Sentimentalism and Naturalism, and could not endure the break with Naturalism; he responded to Sentimentalism in an archaic fashion, accepting its canons uncritically. Indeed, he worked not so much on the revitalizing of Sentimental forms, as on their restoration and reproduction. For this reason Gogol died as an artist-innovator when he fell captive to Sentimentalism.

I cannot develop these general thoughts about Gogol's literary path in greater detail here. To establish them, to reveal all the peripeties of Gogol's struggle with Sentimentalism—his victories over it and his ultimate defeat—and to trace the evolution of the natural style in Gogol's poetics is the subject of a large scholarly study, which I hope to complete in the near future.[29]

Chapter 5

The problem of Gogol's poetics has come to be more and more closely interwoven with the problem of the "Natural School," an issue whose time has come. Formerly the "Natural" style served as a synonym for "Realistic." In view of the broad and undefined nature of the latter term, the very problem of the "Naturalistic" (or "Realistic") school loses its firm historical features. The task of earlier scholars was to delimit Gogol's role in the creation of a "Realistic" trend (which Belinsky and Chernyshevsky had done for him) and to restore that honor to Pushkin and Lermontov.[30] It is clear that from such unfounded assertions the concept of the "Natural School" (and style) spread throughout artistic prose of the nineteenth century. Only K. K. Istomin in his article "The Old Manner of Turgenev," and K. Leontiev in his work on Tolstoi's novels sought to establish the stylistic earmarks of Naturalism from the 40s to the 60s. But Istomin became entangled in the problem of the relationship between Gogol's style and the "Natural" style, going so far as to counterpose them, and he rejected out of hand any concrete definitions of the principles of Naturalist poetics. Leontiev provides an impressive, but incohesive description of the various devices of "Naturalism" without uniting them into a theoretical system. Moreover, he sees Naturalism as a "whole," without any outgrowths, as a static system for the representation of the world frozen in those forms set forth by the genius of Gogol. Nonetheless, a whole series of stylistic devices for the depiction of poses and movements, the material world, and the construction of dialogue is noted by K. Leontiev with remarkable exactitude.

Thus, every student of literature in the mid-nineteenth century encountered the problem of the "Natural" style and the "Natural School".[31]

Interest in Dostoevsky's work, which has reached a peak in recent years, naturally has clashed with the literary murk surrounding the basis of the young Dostoevsky's poetics. Not only has the problem of "Gogolism" surfaced, but something broader—the "Naturalism" of Dostoevsky.[32] The question was posed in an article by A. Beletsky, "Dostoevsky and the Natural School in 1846" (*Science in the Ukraine* [Nauka na Ukraine], 1922, No. 4). Beletsky, however, inclined toward the old substitution of the term "Realism" for the term "Natural School," although it was clear that one ought to speak only about the artistic devices of Gogol's successors in the 40s.

A. Tseitlin found it necessary to speak about "plot structure" in works of the Natural School in his booklet *Tales about Dostoevsky's Poor Civil Servant* (On the History of a Single Plot), 1923. He first makes a series of remarks in passing about the tradition of depicting a "poor civil servant" in the 20s prior to Gogol (Bulgarin, Griboedov's *Woe From Wit*). Then he asserts that Gogol canonized the theme of the poor civil servant, having established only its new "development"; yet he does not reveal what constitutes the novelty of this "development." Nonetheless, that there is a link between Gogol and the works of the 40s-60s seems undoubtable to A. Tseitlin, who finds it "both in the style, especially in the natural style, the embryonic stage of the future Realistic style of the 50s-60s, and in the plot structure and composition." On this basis he also arrogates to himself the right to "examine them outside their chronological sequence in a general analysis." This "general analysis" of the tales of the 40s-60s on the theme of the poor civil servant consists foremost in their classification according to motifs: tales developing the motif of career failures of a civil servant ("The Provincial Woman" by Turgenev [this is a *tale?*— V. V.], "A Fine Person" and "A Strange Story" by Butkov, *An Ordinary Story* by Goncharov, and others); tales with the everyday material of clerical life (Butkov's tale "Trevogin," and others); tales about the family life of a civil servant ("The

Uniform" by Baron Korf, "A Hen-pecked Husband" by P. Mashkov, "A Sweet Wife" by Alexandrov, and others). Among these tales are many stories about the unfortunate love of a poor clerk for some fine young girl: "A Particular Pair" by Butkov, Dal's "Love Till the Grave," and others. In these "Natural" tales the main obstacle to the civil servant's happiness in love is some "significant personage." The appearance on the scene of the significant personage, along with the poor civil servant and the young girl, creates the character trinomial of Dostoevsky's first tales. Tseitlin, quoting journal citations on "Natural" tales about clerks, concentrates entirely upon Dostoevsky's first tales, seeing in them a natural continuation of both the psychological and purely anecdotal tales of the 40s. Of course, the material which Tseitlin excerpted from the journals speaks for itself (however, only where it is successfully demonstrated). Tseitlin not only deprives the theory of the "Natural School's" plot of its historical perspective and inner dynamics (indeed, he treats it "outside a chronological sequence"), he also schematicizes it to an extreme. While the theme of the poor civil servant undoubtedly was one of the central themes of Naturalism, and the common motifs of its development indicated by Tseitlin were the notable parts of its story frame, nonetheless it is impossible to distinguish a "Natural" tale from the adjacent genres in other literary schools on the basis of these features. And Tseitlin himself becomes entangled in the question of the limits and earmarks of the "Natural School". For this reason, the only firm conclusion in his work is one which is hinted at in all the journal citations of the 40s-50s: that Naturalism's favorite hero was the civil servant in the various spheres of his life—social and domestic.

I set about the investigation of Gogol's influence in my article, "The Plot and Architectonics of Dostoevsky's Novel *Poor Folk* in Connection with the Question of the Poetics of the Natural School." In the article I set forth in detail the usual judgments about Naturalism's artistic dependence upon Gogol and attempted to reproduce concretely those literary tendencies of the 30s and 40s which were created under the influence of Gogol's stylistic manner. I elucidated the general farcical tendency of novellas in the 30s among Gogol's successors, who took his "The Tale of Two Ivans," "The Nose," and, less often, "Notes of a Madman" as models; they imitated *The Inspector General* in organizing their conversational language styles; the farce was interwoven with the anecdote. Many of these writers combined imitation of Gogol directly with adherence to contrasting artistic forms, for example, the Sentimental-Romantic, and the philosophical-society types (Mashkov, Voskresensky, and others), at times stitching one and the same work together from pieces of varying stylistic construction. By the 40s this genre receded into the background; writers struggled against it. The anecdote, by way of contrast, remained in the foreground. But now it was a means of creating images of civil servants, usurers, acquisitive types, and petty landowners with a single "fervor" and "passion," or contradictory qualities. The artistic images become oxymoronic and complex; they are cloaked in a net of moral and civil clichés. The general stylistic forms change. Gogol remains at the center of attention, but the choice of his works as objects of imitation is made differently. *Dead Souls*, and later "The Overcoat," become the basis of Naturalism's artistic quests.

Another tendency is interwoven with this, one which proceeds immediately from and is related to Gogol but which has another artistic genesis—the "physiological" or "documentary style." Some of its representatives (like Dal) had only the barest connection with Gogol, but set off on a course of the "documentation" of nature parallel to Gogol, more interacting with him than depending upon him. For this reason, the stylistic basis of the advocates of this tendency differs from that of Gogol. The basis of the tale or "sketch" is not the anecdote, but ethnographic, everyday, sociological material which, of course, is sometimes spiced with anecdotal "scenes from nature," but only episodically. In the mid-40s there was no hostility between these tendencies. But a new synthetic tendency temporarily gained supremacy. This tendency, originating in Gogol's "The Overcoat," heralded the synthesis of Naturalistic and Sentimental forms, and began to restore, albeit in a new style, the Sentimental genres. Dostoevsky, the leader of this movement, sought to achieve an organic adaptation to the "Natural" style of both the Romantic Hoffmannesque style (*The Double*) and the style of Romantic-horror ("The Landlady"). In a word, Dostoevsky's aim was, it would seem, to pass through the very same stages through which Gogol had passed, but to set off against his forms the forms of renovated Naturalism.

This, in essence, was the framework of my ideas when I began my article on *Poor Folk*. It was necessary to narrow their development somewhat, confining myself to one current of Naturalism, on whose crest *Poor Folk* had been raised. Lately my understanding of the evolution of Naturalism in the 40s and 50s has deepened. I shall briefly and systematically summarize its core here.

Gogol did not overcome the contradictions concealed in the contrasting methods—Natural and Sentimental— in the artistic perception of the same objects. Of course, their synthesis generally was possible; and one branch of Naturalism realized the legacy of its leader. The varieties of the Sentimental genre were adapted to the Naturalistic manner of depiction. A displacement in points of view took place, and the perception of the world is refracted through the prism of an interpolated narrator, a "poor man." This is precisely what Dostoevsky did; Yakov Butkov, Mikhail Dostoevsky, Alexander Palma and others followed a similar course. Even Turgenev paid his due to these trends (Petushkov, in the play *The Bachelor*), but like Dostoevsky he smoothed out the traits of the skaz, while remaining within the limits of the same devices of depiction and the same plot structure. It is only natural that the principle of combining Natural and Sentimental poetics could have been realized in different fashions. Even moribund Romantic forms were resurrected and infused into the basic Naturalistic core. Subsequently, all of these tendencies swept aside by Gogol were categorized as the "Pushkinian" element; not only Turgenev, but Goncharov and Dostoevsky as well, dreamed about combining it with the Gogolian element. One may say that these writers pursued various courses in their own work while subordinating themselves to the same impulse. Yet since purely "Gogolian" stylistic forms continued to be preserved in the poetics of Naturalist-physiologists like Pisemsky, Ostrovsky and others, advocates of a synthesis gradually began to disassociate themselves also from the Gogolian style, transforming it or assigning to it solely the humble role of depicting "lower" comic types. The stylistic principles which had developed in this group were varied, and essentially incompatible, but in the literary-philistine consciousness they received the common label "Realistic." All the same, Naturalism and Realism are hostile, albeit not opposite, tendencies.

Another line of the "Natural School" rejected the pathetic element in Gogol, as well as his Sentimental strivings, seeing in them a reversion to routine, to vanquished, antiquated fashions (cf. Pisemsky's article on *Dead Souls*). Excepting the pathetic passages, the first volume of *Dead Souls* was considered the central work by representatives of this literary group. An adherence to Gogol's conversational-language style was the basic requirement in the poetics of this tendency. Apollon Grigoriev regarded Pisemsky as the leader of this group. He wrote that Pisemsky was alloted the new manner in transforming reality, but he did not succeed in saying anything new about it. When his view of art was expressed with particular clarity, as in "The Comedian," he can be seen to be a direct successor to Gogol, though in this as in other works he is only half of this great teacher.[33] Pisemsky renounced Gogol's "subjective" manner, third-person skaz (although there is not, properly speaking, any skaz in *Dead Souls*), and the hyperbole of expressions and images, which to a significant degree were created by the grimaces of the narrator. And Apollon Grigoriev explains the difference between Pisemsky and Gogol by showing that Pisemsky's relationship to reality was subordinate and dependent, whereas Gogol's was absolutely free: that of a creative genius. Mikhailov, Menshikov, and others may be considered akin to Pisemsky in this series. This branch of Naturalism was created in interaction with the genre of physiological sketches, which originally comprised a variegated stylistic mix, but were closest of all to the Naturalistic tendency headed by Dal.

The relationship between Dal and Gogol was complex. Dal initially was considered (in a humorous survey, of course) the father of the "bast-sandal school." But as his circle of plots and the scope of his "nature" expanded, he ceased to be distinguishable from the "Naturalists" in the general literary consciousness. The elevating of Dal to the rank of a writer of the "Natural School", however, was accompanied by such peculiar circumstances that one is forced to speak of a literary group aligned with him in particular. The fact is that at the onset of the 40s Dal and his devices of depiction were still acceptable to fervent opponents of Gogolian Naturalism (for example, his sketch "The Ural Cossack" in the collection *Ours, Copied from Nature*, 1842). Somehow he borrowed from Gogol without subordinating himself to him; he went alongside Gogol in search of "nature as it is," and even influenced him. "Each of his lines teaches and enlightens me, bringing me closer to an understanding of the Russian way of life, our folk ways," wrote Gogol.

Meanwhile, as Dal was aligning himself more closely with the basic core of the "Natural School", Belinsky was inclined to see a turning point in this affiliation. "Tell me," he said, "which of his former tales may be reread after, for example, 'Sausage-makers and Bearded Men', a tale by Lugansky, a writer who is not from the new generation, but who is gifted and, fortunately, has abandoned his old, false tendency for a new and better one."[34]

Dal gravitated toward the variegated mass of physiological sketches, in a few of which, moreover, could be seen the clear traces of Gogol's style. Proponents of this tendency also rejected skaz on principle, although they sometimes practiced it, cultivating complex forms of professional, everyday conversational language, insisting on "statistics" and a documentary style. In essence, this was the "second Natural School" of which Apollon Grigoriev had spoken.

Of course, it would be possible to establish many smaller subdivisions. Indeed, none of the more or less major writers directly copied Gogol's style, rather they sought to transform and synthesize it with other artistic forms. There were many accumulated yet separable layers even from the old epoch rejected by Gogol. However, the presence in a writer's work of various peculiarities of the Gogolian style or proximate "dirty" devices and "low plot structures" was a criterion for considering a writer part of the "Natural School." Such was the case even though the entire Gogolian "Natural" element could be combined with forms that were alien to his poetics.

Until the end of the 50s Gogol was viewed as a leader. His works were seen as objects of imitation or as things to be surpassed; new stylistic designs were sketched on the Gogolian canvas. Those who departed from Gogolian poetics carried elements of it along with them (Turgenev, Sologub, and others); those who wanted to assume the role of leader by surpassing Gogol, developed his artistic tendencies further (Dostoevsky). The "Natural School" did not die without a trace in the 50s. Its poetics passed into new artistic systems with new functions, adapting itself to a new basic formal-aesthetic pivot (cf. the petty bureaucrats in the late novels of Fyodor Dostoevsky, Gogolian devices in Turgenev's negative character portrayals, in Goncharov, and such like). The "documentary style" as an outgrowth of "Naturalism" began to form an independent artistic tendency. Pisemsky, Grigorovich, and others in later years relished Gogol's artistic devices. Yet all this does not define the basic tone. The end of the 50s marked the victory of "Realism" in its various outgrowths and meanings over "Naturalism." The turn toward Realism is most vividly expressed in Dostoevsky's novel *The Village of Stepanchikovo and Its Inhabitants*. In this work the twofold artistic division is immediately sensed and can be easily demonstrated.

October 25, 1924   Viktor Vinogradov

Notes

1. Though without any particularly original ideas, these writers have written about Mandelshtam's book: P. Morozov in *Mir Bozhii,* 1902, No. 2; A. Lipovskii in *Gogolevskii sbornik izdatel'stva russkoi biblioteki Sibiri,* 1902. A. Gornfeld, *Russkoe bogatstvo,* 1902, no. 1; N. Korobka in *Zhurnal Ministerstva narodnogo prosveshcheniia,* 1904, V.

2. Pushkin who "is the real founder of the *Natural School,* is always faithful to the nature of man and faithful to his fate."

3. In the article "Kak proizoshel tip Akakiia Akakievicha," where Gogol's work, on the basis of the original edition of "Shinel'" ("The Overcoat") is observed from this point of view.

4. *Vesy,* 1909, No. 4, and then reprinted in the book: *Lug Zelenyi.*

5. *Apollon,* 1911, No. 8.

6. The same characteristic of the Gogolian style is treated somewhat differently in *Kniga otrazhenii* (*1906*)—*Problema gogolevskogo iumora*: '*Nos' i 'Portret'.*

7. Vasilii Gippius's book *Gogol'* (1924) is closely aligned to the aesthetico-psychological position of the Symbolists. Yet since it seeks to synthesize all the achievements of Gogoliana and presents an entire schema of Gogol's aesthetical evolution, it is more appropriate to discuss it separately.

8. I likewise am not mentioning Ivan Ermakov's *Ocherki po psikhologii tvorchestva N. V. Gogolia.*

9. Viktor Shklovskii's "Tristram Shendi i teoriia romana." Cf. V. M. Zhirmunskii's review in *Nachalo,* 1921, no. 1. V. Vinogradov's "Siuzhet i kompozitsiia povesti Gogolia 'Nos'." *Nachalo,* no. 1 (1921). Boris Eikhenbaum, *Lermontov,* 1924. The chapter on Lermontov's prose.

10. "Marksisty i formal'nyi metod," *Lef.* 1923, No. 3.

11. *Rodnoi iazyk v shkole,* 1923, No. 4.

12. *Khristianskaia mysl',* 1916, nos. 1, 3, 5, 6, 7-8, 10, 12.

13. Lukoianovskii's article in the anthology: *Besedy. Sbornik Obshchestva istorii literatury v Moskve.* Edited by N. V. Iakovlev.

14. Cf. V. V. Danilov's "Dedushka russkikh istoricheskikh zhurnalov." *Istoricheskii vestnik,* 1915, No. 7. Cf. also his "N. V. Gogol' i P. P. Svinin." *Russkii filologicheskii vestnik,* 1915, No. 1.

15. *Beseay. Sbornik Obshchestva istorii literatury,* 1945.

16. The "canvas of conception" of "Dva Ivana" is compared throughout to "Povest' o tom, kak possorilis' Ivan Ivanovich s Ivanom Nikiforovichem."

17. *Izvestiia Otdela russkogo iazyka i slovesnosti Rossiiskoi Akademii Nauk,* vol. XXIV, book I, 1919.

18. *Russkii filologicheskii vestnik,* 1917, nos. 1-2.

19. A review of the two Stender-Petersen articles is in the journal *Slavia,* R. Sesit, 4, 1924.

20. I shall cite a few examples:
Osip says: "I feel like eating the whole world."
Merimée translates: "Je parie que tout le monde a déjà
                    dîné à cette heure."
Dobchinsky: "eyes as quick as little beasts, such that
             they even embarrass one."
Merimée: "Le regarde comme s'il avait le diable au corps."
Khlestakov: You know, I spent everything on the road."
Merimée: "J'ai été retenu en route."

21. See Trubitsyn's *O narodnoi poezii v obshchestvennom i literaturnom obikhode pervoi treti XIX v.,* St. Petersburg, 1912.

22. *Severnye tsvety* ("Northern Flowers") for 1830.

23. The almanac: *Sirota*, 1831.

24. *Moskovskii Telegraf,* 1829, vol. XXVIII. "O roli Val'ter-Skotta v literature XX godov." General information may be drawn from the works of Zamotin, *Romantizm 20 godov,* vol II; I. Trubitsyn's work *O narodnoi poezii;* and N. K. Kozmin's *Ocherki iz istorii russkogo romantizma.*

25. I examine in detail the problems of Walter Scott, the tradition created by him on Russian soil, the influence of Russian "Walter Scotts," and the direct influence of Walter Scott on Gogol in the work "Val'ter-Skott i Gogol," which I shall earmark for the *Zeitschrift für slavische Philologie* published in Leipzig under the editorship of M. R. Vasmer.

26. My article "Gogol' i Jules Janin" in *Literaturnaia Mysl'*, no. 3 is devoted to the question of Jules Janin's influence on Gogol.

27. In my work "Gogol' i romanticheski-uzhasnyi zhanr" I discuss in detail the genre of Romantic-horror and its Russian offshoots, Gogol's attitude toward it, and his "struggle" with Frenetic poetics.

28. Cf. my article: "Siuzhet i kompozitsiia povesti Gogolia 'Nos' " in the journal *Nachalo*, no. 1.

29. Bibliographical information in the literature of Gogol studies may be found in the surveys of S. Bertenson in *Izvestiia Otdela russkogo iazyka i slovesnosti Rossiikoi Akademii Nauk.* Petrograd. 1917, vol. XXII, book I and in Vladislavlev's index (Leningrad, 1924). I have added the article by Rodzevich and the works of Stender-Petersen.

30. It is sufficient to mention such works as Orest Miller's "Sushchnost' Gogolevskogo napravleniia" in *Russkaia literatura posle Gogolia,* Petersburg, 1875; Barkhin's: "O Gogolevskom napravlenii," *Filologicheskie zapiski*, 1908, no. 1; Shenrok's: "Kto byl rodonachal'nikom real'nogo napravleniia v nashei literature" in *Russkaia Starina*, 1892, no. 2; Konstantin V. Mochulskii's: "Chto zaveshchal Gogol' sozdannoi im natural'noi shkole" in *Sbornik Novorossiiskogo Universiteta,* Odessa, 1909, and such like.

31. Especially those doing research upon Gogol's influence upon later writers. Cf. A. Zmorovich "O iazyke i stile proizvedenii Mel'nikova-Pecherskogo" in *Russkii filologicheskii vestnik*, 1916, nos. 1-2.

32. V. F. Pereverzev, *Tvorchestvo Dostoevskogo*, 1912; Iu. Tynianov,

"Dostoevsky i Gogol'," 1922; V. Vinogradov, "Stil' peterburgskoi poemy Dostoevskogo *Dvoinik.*"

33. Ap. Grigoriev's *Russkaia Literatura v seredine XIX v, Sobranie sochinenii* pod redaktsiei V. P. Savodnika, fascicle. 9, p. 50.

34. A review of Count V. A. Sollogub's book: *Na son griadushchii. Otryvki iz vsednevnoi zhizni.* vol. 1. Siberia, 1844.

OHIO UNIVERSITY LIBRARY

Please return this book as so
have finished with it. In ord